SEXUALITY AT WORK

(HOW DOES IT AFFECT YOU?)

SEXUALITY AT WORK

(HOW DOES IT AFFECT YOU?)

JEAN CIVIL

B. T. BATSFORD LIMITED · LONDON

Batsford Business Online: www.batsford.com

© Jean Civil 1998
First published 1998

Published by BT Batsford Ltd,
583 Fulham Road,
London SW6 5BY

Batsford Business Online: www.batsford.com

Printed by
Redwood Books
Trowbridge
Wiltshire

All rights reserved. No part of this publication may be reproduced, stored in a retrieval system, or transmitted in any form or by any means, electronic, electrical chemical, optical, photocopying, recording or otherwise without the prior permission of the publisher.

ISBN 0 7134 8370 9

A CIP catalogue record for this book
is available from The British Library

CONTENTS

Acknowledgements	11
Preface	13
Abstract	15
Introduction	17
Chapter 1 Motives for the research	**21**
As a management trainer	22
As a senior manager	25
As a counsellor	27
Introduction to the research	31
Chapter 2 What is sexuality?	**33**
Chapter 3 What has been said about sexuality at work	**41**
Sexuality in organizations	50
What influences the way in which managers are affected by their sexuality at work?	53
Chapter 4 Early sexual messages and experiences	**57**
Personal questionnaire	57
Introduction	59
Early sexual messages	59
Female managers	60
Male managers	63
Attitude change: do managers still carry their early sexual messages?	73

First sexual experience	80
The women	82
The men	87

Chapter 5 Managers' perceptions about sexuality at work — **93**

What are the sexual messages at work	93
What are the stories of sexuality at work?	106
What aspects of working life are identified where sexuality does affect the managers?	117

Chapter 6 Case studies — **131**

1. Nick – naughty but nice	132
2. Vivienne – vivacious but virtuous	139
3. Steve – swinging Sixties scene	147
4. Pru-prudish passion	152
5. Andy – angry and aware	157
6. Fiona – father couldn't be nearer	161
7. Paul – positively promoted	164
8. Hilary – horrible to happy	167
9. Bryan – beauty and the beast	171
10. Chris – cocooned and cautious	177

Chapter 7 Discussion and conclusions — **187**

What aspects of sexuality emerged from the research?	187
The effect of the research on me	195
The practical significance of this research	202
Conclusion	205

Chapter 8 So what? How does this affect me as a manager? — **209**

Further Reading — **231**

Index — **237**

FIGURES

Figure	Description	Page
1	Management hierarchy	145
2	Dialectical research cycle (after Rowan and Reason 1981)	198
3	My research cycle showing my research process	199
4	Model of competence steps	200

TABLES

Table	Description	Page
1	Analysis of sexual messages	72
2	Attitude changes and conflict – differences between men and women	80
3	Summary of first sexual experiences	91
4	Analysis of sexual messages at work	106
5	Sexual stories of managers – shared and separate experiences	117
6	How sexuality affects managers at work	127
7a	Analysis of sexual messages	128
7b	Attitude changes	128
7c	Summary of first sexual experiences	129
7d	Perceived sexual messages at work	129
7e	Sexual stories at work were about...	130
7f	How sexuality affects managers at work	130

To Geoff

My friend, my comedian, my lover, my husband.

ACKNOWLEDGEMENTS

I would like to thank all the people who took part in this research, for their honesty, and for entrusting me with confidential and sometimes painful experiences. My thanks go to my husband Geoff and my son Carl, who tried to make me laugh in times of self doubt, and to Dee Wood who helped to produce the final version, to Brenda Mallon for her comments on the contents and to Judi Marshall and Steve Fineman who supervised me in the initial academic research methods and investigations. Thanks also to John Winters for his guidance in rewriting the research into a book. Also a big thank you to all my close friends who supported me, helped me to believe that my research was worthwhile, and encouraged me to finish it and publish this book.

PREFACE

It cannot be proved! It does not exist! There is no research with which to compare the findings in this work! Why hasn't someone else written about it before? These are some of the more printable comments made during seven years of research into the ways in which sexuality affects managers at work. It is fortunate that these responses were in the minority, for it was the opposite views that inspired me to continue with the daunting prospect of lifting the huge boulder that had concealed the frantic sexual interplay in the workplace.

Views like 'You must publish your findings because everyone knows that sex is rife in the workplace!' 'So many of our management decisions and changes are based on who fancies who and who feels sexually threatened by whom!' 'Our strategic plan and management restructuring was based on who slept with whom; mind you, it has been the same wherever I have worked!'

After such comments it was difficult not to be encouraged to publish these stories involving sex and gender which invoke such strong feelings of anger, jealousy and envy about many aspects of work, such as lovers going off with someone else, lack of promotion, or meteoric rises to positions of power.

> *'Jealousy is between three people where the other person may take away someone I want whilst envy is between two people where another person has something I want'* **Nancy Friday [9]**

PREFACE

As you read this book it is highly likely that you will have at least one 'ah ha!' experience – when you suddenly make a connection between something that has happened to you in the past which explains why you adopt your present attitude or behaviour. I doubt if you will be able to read through the various stories told later without reflecting on your own sexual messages and experiences. I hope that Chapter 8 will enable those of you who have a line management responsibility to understand how your sexuality affects the people you manage and also how other people's sexuality needs managing.

ABSTRACT

About the research

This study encapsulates the phenomenon of sexuality at work. It highlights how early sexual messages given to children can be recalled and how in many cases these messages continue to influence people as adults within organizations.

The research is based on the findings of 402 senior managers (201 male and 201 female). They managed in both open and closed organizations (closed being managers working in prisons). These findings draw attention to the need for further research in this daunting area, despite the dearth of previous qualitative studies. In parallel, the study explores if and how managers are affected by their sexuality at work and concludes that sexuality does affect the vast majority of managers at work, in organizations. The study is multi-faceted and is divided into three sections.

Firstly, early sexual attitudes and sexual experiences are explored and categorised. Then I identify if people's attitudes towards sexuality has changed since their early years or if their early sexual attitudes create inner conflict.

Secondly, managers reveal how their sexuality affects them at work, in interviews, in meetings, in promotions and in relationships. These categories, among others, emerged through empathic interviewing and were supported by perceived organizational messages and stories.

Thirdly, the research selects ten cases which enrich the study.

ABSTRACT

Managers highlighted different aspects in this research. Illustrations are given of how early sexual messages may affect managers at work; how sexuality may affect decisions at interviews; how sexual feelings or early sexual experiences can be projected on to other staff; how sexuality affects relationships between colleagues and how confidentiality can be affected by sexual liaisons at work.

INTRODUCTION

I have written this book for all managers and those who are managed. Although it will concentrate on managers at work, it will also be pertinent for managers at home.

We are sexual beings, and to deny our sexuality is to deny part of ourselves.

Regardless of your position in the organization, your role, status, gender, culture, or sexual orientation, there will be times when your sexual feelings will be aroused to a greater or lesser degree. Do you agree or disagree with this statement?

Begin by simply thinking about your experience of interviews, either what you have heard about them or those in which you have been involved. Comments such as 'Never mind the qualifications, just appoint the gorgeous one', 'Having someone like that around the place will certainly liven things up around here,' have been heard in the past but maybe not so often in today's climate. Officially, such comments must not be made, but in many workplaces they still occur. Perhaps you have made a similar statement or thought along those lines.

Since concern has grown about equal opportunities in interviews, more managers have been nervous of voicing their opinion on how they feel or think about candidates. However, no comment voiced does not necessarily mean there is no connection. You could still be thinking subjectively about the candidate.

You know that you are drawn to some people and withdraw or disconnect from others, and any sexual attraction would be unlikely to be discussed for fear of retribution. Although that is the official

INTRODUCTION

line, as a manager or someone who is managed, you may still feel attracted to certain individuals.

There can be many reasons for this. Maybe their 'shadows' remind you of people you have liked or disliked. Or it could be that their religion coincides or is at odds with your own beliefs. Perhaps their race or gender make you feel comfortable or uncomfortable. Their values may or may not be shared. Equally their sexual orientation may play a part in how you respond to them. Possibly their physical appearance can affect how you feel. Or you may be sexually attracted to someone because of your individual physical chemistry and own psychological needs and self-talk. All of these factors are likely to affect how you feel, either positively or negatively. Remember, feelings are facts!

Whatever the reasons for your being sexually attracted to some people but not to others, you still need to be aware of how your behaviour can affect the people with whom you work. It is not good enough to say that what you do in your private life is nothing to do with work colleagues. Normally it isn't, but it is a concern if you bring personal issues to affect, by your liaisons or your behaviour, others in the workplace.

Managing people and being managed is difficult enough without the added complication of having to cover certain actions by resorting to subterfuge. This is not to say that you should never get involved, but simply highlights the need for yours and others sexuality to be recognised as a significant force that can motivate and demotivate staff.

So how can you benefit from this book? Firstly, I suggest that early recalled sexual messages can affect individuals at work and advocate that people need to recognise their own sexual messages and that if they consider that these are causing them difficulties at work they are encouraged to change them. Thus you may become more aware of your own early messages and either be pleased about this awareness or you may choose to change them.

INTRODUCTION

You *can* change the sexual messages that you no longer want to carry with you through life and break free from the control they have over you. However, many of you may say 'I can't'. In this case you should exchange the word 'Cant' for 'Won't': you won't change; it's not that you can't. Can't implies an inability to be able to do so, whereas won't is a refusal to try to change. By changing destructive attitudes and messages you will free yourself to live a fuller and more rewarding life. This will enable you to be able to see a clearer picture of yourself and others. When you change negative self-talk into positive self-talk it will be like removing contaminated roots and replacing them with healthy ones.

How can I change, you may ask. Well, begin by recalling your early sexual messages. Then look to see if there is any connection with the way in which you now think, feel or behave at work. You may be pleased with some of the recollections but if you were given negative sexual messages and want to change them, complete the process by reprogramming your thinking to a more positive and enabling way of thinking, feeling or behaving.

Secondly, you may benefit from reading the stories related to me by managers about their experiences of sexuality in the workplace. This will offer you the opportunity of questioning whether your sexuality affects you at work in similar ways when you read how 402 senior managers responded to questions about their sexuality at work and how it affected them.

However, before you begin to read these findings, let me pose some questions. Does your sexuality affect you at work? Yes or No?

1. Do you look forward to Monday morning to see a loved one at work?
2. Do you avoid someone you once loved?
3. Do you enjoy certain meetings where a certain person to whom you are attracted will be present?

INTRODUCTION

4. Are there situations at work where you feel uncomfortable because a lover or an 'ex' is present?
5. Have you ever been appointed to a new position because of a sexual involvement with one of the senior managers on the selection panel?
6. Have you ever been promoted by someone with whom you have been sexually involved?
7. Have you ever appointed someone to whom you are sexually attracted?
8. Have you ever avoided appointing someone for fear of becoming sexually involved with them?
9. Does someone at work excite you sexually?
10. Have you ever been sexually involved with someone with whom you work?

If you answered 'yes' to any one of the above questions then it is likely that your sexuality affects you at work.

Perhaps it is time that we started addressing or considering these questions rather than turning a blind eye by pretending that workplace sexuality does not exist. For, as Eliza Collins [32] observed, 'In the long run, the most fragile thing is probably not the corporation or the people, but the love relationship itself.'

Thirdly, I hope you will benefit from the final chapter that offers you many suggestions as to how you can manage your own and others' sexuality at work. I will offer ways in which you can use these findings in order to manage yourself and your colleagues more effectively.

Fourthly, you may benefit from the fact that this study has an underlying counselling approach and so you may find that some of the ways in which people have been able to react on their new awareness will help you.

CHAPTER 1

MOTIVES FOR THE RESEARCH

There were three reasons for undertaking this research, all stemming from my own experiences at work. Firstly, as a management trainer, I heard how sexuality was affecting managers at work in terms of their roles, status, gender, sexual orientation and relationships. Secondly, as a senior manager, I had witnessed peoples' sexuality affecting them in interviews, meetings, team-teaching, decision-making, problem-solving, delegation, gender and power struggles and in their relationships with both sexes; and thirdly as a counsellor, I worked with many clients whose concerns or issues varied, but who revealed during the therapeutic process how their sexuality was a cause of stress for them both at home and at work.

What had happened in these three work settings to motivate me to undertake research into the daunting area of managers' sexual attitudes and behaviours at work? It is daunting because sexuality is 'private and often kept secret in organizations and elsewhere' [6]. People do not readily share their experiences and sexuality is a topic which arouses many different emotions: feelings of guilt, anger, joy, shame, fear, embarrassment and sometimes loss. Researching sexuality requires sensitivity, empathic interviewing and counselling skills, and demands complete confidentiality, in order to protect the subjects of the research from being identified.

As a management trainer

I worked at the Staff College (now replaced by the Further Education Development Agency) which was a national management training college for further and higher education, and for ten years I was a tutor on numerous courses which came under the general heading of 'Managing People Skills'. Later I worked as a freelance management trainer in business, commerce, industrial and medical settings. As a trainer I met and taught managers from all over the British Isles and some overseas visitors. It was in this capacity that I heard so many stories of sexuality at work, some of which are recorded in this research. This work involved me in a wide range of specialities including stress management, interpersonal skills, HIV, personal growth for managers, women into management, team building, assertiveness for men, advanced counselling skills and consultancies with senior management teams. During my time as a management trainer people shared many of their sexual concerns with me; these included impotence, premature ejaculation, frigidity, barrenness, losing power at work, sexless relationships, homosexual and bisexual fears of coming out, childlessness, affairs, loss of libido, being HIV positive and stress-related illnesses resulting from their sexuality.

I encountered homosexuals who shared their fears about 'coming out' and the consequent reactions of their employers, colleagues, staff, students and sometimes partners (if bisexual), towards them. I recall working with one group which included a man who was devastated to discover his son was gay, whilst elsewhere another younger man had just told his parents that he was homosexual. Bringing these two people together, with their permission, helped them to overcome their feelings of isolation from their individual families.

There were men who were afraid to show their feelings, or to comment on women's behaviour or appearance, for fear of being labelled sexist. Men who found the equal opportunity policies difficult to handle because their childhood role models of women as mothers were so far removed from their female career colleagues. Some talked of their inner conflict about the women with whom they worked, saying that they found their female colleagues sexually exciting and intellectually stimulating, but were afraid to show any emotion toward them and often felt uncomfortable in their presence. Communication with the opposite sex was also an issue for some men, who believed that their actions were supportive of women, but could not convincingly express themselves. They frequently felt vulnerable and hurt by the abrasive responses they received from some women. A number of recent incidents emphasise this point.

David Thomas, Editor of *Punch*, spoke on television in 1991 of the nagging feelings that exist between men and women now that feminism is firmly entrenched. He did not object to the 'feminine' but to the 'ism' – the extreme ideology. He referred to the article 'Bad Mouthing' (*Sunday Times* 1990) which stated that while it is permissible for women to make comments about men, the reverse is taboo. This particular article was referred to by the men with whom I worked in 1992 on an inaugural conference 'Assertiveness for Men'. The *Sunday Mirror* commented on this course before it took place under a 'Would you believe it?' column; the thought that men might need assertiveness training was seen as a joke. Unfortunately many people confuse assertiveness with aggressiveness. Nevertheless, these 18 men very soon shared their innermost concerns about their sexuality; they commented on the course evaluation forms and in person to myself and also my male colleague that the reason they could be open and honest was thanks to the absence of women who might jump on them because of their unintended sexist comments.

MOTIVES FOR RESEARCH

Another comment was that they might have played sexual macho games if women had been present.

As well as working with all-male groups I was also involved with numerous all-female groups. These women were attending Women into Management conferences. Whilst the issue of gender has been well documented, there is a dearth of knowledge and research about how sexuality affects management work. As I was the only woman tutor at the Staff College for three years I was able to identify with many of the gender issues that the women raised. Women talked freely about their rise to senior management, where promotion was almost always accompanied by comments relating their success to their sleeping habits. Many senior women managers talk about the stress of having to deal with an all-male senior management team and particularly having to cope with their innuendoes, jokes and patronising remarks. Some women shared the difficulties of their sexuality at work: how their sexual involvement with managers had led them into leaving their job; how they could not share their sexual orientation with other members of staff; or how previous liaisons with a man or woman in some departmental organization created stress for them at meetings.

Many women raised the issue of the different roles they had: wife, mother, single parent, stepmother, daughter, lover, sister and career woman. Men have similar multiple roles, but few mentioned them in terms of their gender difficulties as a manager. Working on both male and female single-sex courses, I noted many differences in management style and attitudes, but I found little difference between the sexes with reference to sexuality. My experience was that they both shared the same fundamental need to be loved and to have a loving sexual relationship. Many delegates of both sexes who attended these courses had been badly damaged by previous sexual experiences; some had experienced abuse, rape, incest or violence. Some had been damaged psychologically by broken relationships, leaving them with feelings of guilt, rejection, abandonment or anger. There were men and women who hated the opposite sex because their own relationships had ended in hurt, rejection or feelings of betrayal.

There were stories from both sexes of how affairs had affected their working and home lives, whether their lovers were inside or outside the workplace. Some delegates related how the affairs of senior managers had affected them and other colleagues; of staff who would not speak to each other because lovers had changed partners; partners at work who created problems when an affair had reached crisis level and colleagues were taking sides; and the problems created by staff leaving their wife or husband for someone at work. I have also heard and still hear so many stories, as a management trainer, about the difficulties people experience in coping at work when they are highly stressed about their sexuality.

As a senior manager

I first became interested in the hypothesis that sexuality might affect managers at work when I was the only woman in an all-male senior management team in 1979. That particular college was a monotechnic building college where the ethos was very patriarchal. There was only one other woman on the academic staff, a first level lecturer. When I went for my interview and asked a tutor where the principal's room was, his response was that the interviews for a secretary had been held the previous day! As the only woman out of eight people being interviewed, I was offered the post as head of a new department for general and community education. On returning to my college after the interview, delighted with my result, a female colleague said 'That's one in the eye for women's lib.' I was surprised at this reaction. It was only later that I realised just how true this statement was. At the time it did not register with me that it would be a difficulty I would have to overcome. Until then my gender had been an advantage to me in the world of counselling with all the sexual stereotyping surrounding counselling and caring.

At this inner city college I encountered sexual bullying from some male colleagues. As part of my job description was to introduce community education in this college, I put up posters which were then ripped down. I was challenged on my first staff appointment (a woman) on the grounds that she had been appointed because she was one of the 'counselling female softies' who had no place in an all-male environment. Community education meant allowing women into the building, so lavatories had to be provided and room layouts were changed from desks facing the tutors to chairs placed in circles. Women came into the building and were looked at as though they were something from another planet. All these changes created a lot of anxiety and sexual innuendoes were rife. At management meetings there would be discussions about interviews, short listing women, and detrimental comments about the 'Ms' factor on application forms. When we were discussing managerial issues sexual feelings were often raised covertly and overtly. Fortunately I was working with a Principal who was very supportive and who backed me in all the developments that I undertook over the three years I was there.

When I moved to my next college as the head of the Health Department, I was again the only woman, but now with nine men on a senior management team. Sexuality was still an issue on many occasions but this time there were three male colleagues who spoke up on behalf of women and would take other men to task about their sexist comments. The Principal of this college, when newly appointed, had asked the caretaker to remove some female nude pictures from his wall. As a result it quickly reverberated around the college that here was someone who did not approve of such practices.

Over the years that I worked with many male senior managers both inside and outside the college, I learned a great deal about them, their values and belief systems, their sexual feelings about colleagues, and their difficulties in relating to some female, and male, staff. Some would talk confidentially about the problem of working with women with whom they had been sexually involved. Others talked of their difficulties in meetings when sexually attractive women or men were present. Two admitted that they avoided certain parts of the college, on inspection visits, so they would not see a specific colleague with whom they had been sexually involved.

At the same time they would discuss their managerial style, how they believed that sexuality never played a part in their decision making, and how they believed that their staff saw them. Their own perceptions varied enormously from how their staff did see them. One manager saw himself as an objective man who did not let the fact that a member of staff was female influence him at all in the way he thought or behaved. Some of his female staff named him the 'preying mantis', they did not want to be alone with him in his room and many of them saw him as a sexually frustrated chauvinist. Stories were rife within this environment about people being promoted because of sexual liaisons and of women being given jobs at interview because of their sexual attractiveness. As a senior manager I became aware of just how much psychic energy was being used up in the whole area of both positive and negative sexual relationships.

As a counsellor

I have worked as a counsellor since 1969, during which time I have become aware of just how much stress and anxiety is due to people's difficulties with their sexual feelings and behaviour. Among other approaches, I found that looking at people's early childhood messages often proved a useful tool with which to work. When I trained as a counsellor I became familiar with a number of different theoretical counselling approaches including Rogerian [29, 42, 43], Gestalt [28], Rational Emotive Therapy (RET) [3], Neuro Linguistic Programming (NLP) [61], Art Therapy, Psychodrama and

Transactional Analysis (TA) [1, 2]. Some of these actually contradict each other, but their frameworks have proved useful to different clients, as well as being part of the syllabus for the counselling courses I tutored. It is the theory of transactional analysis, along with many other theories, that offers the probability that early childhood messages can affect people in later life. During my training in transactional analysis (1978), I completed a record of my own messages on different aspects of my own life, including money, education, parental behaviour, marriage, religion, success, birth and sexual messages. I realised how powerful these messages were, and I was able to understand the attitudes I subsequently held in all these areas. As a result I became a convert to this approach which was reinforced by the experience of seeing clients gaining from their exploration of early messages.

I first became interested in the theory of early recalled messages in the late Fifties when I was training to be a nursery nurse. During my training the health tutor said 'battered babies grow up to batter their own babies.' I thought this unbelievable – surely if one was battered as a child, then that experience must have been so awful that the memory of it would mean that no one as a parent would ever want to re-inflict such horrors onto their own child. I did not argue with the tutor as I was young, inexperienced and in those days believed everything I was told. The sad fact is that what she said is actually, true: research has shown that people continue to play out their messages on their children.

In later years in the Sixties I worked as a counsellor with people who were dependent on drugs, that is to say they used non-medically prescribed drugs. Recently when updating my work with addicts, my thoughts about early messages were reinforced. When I was working with individuals 25 years ago I found that they had experienced similar childhood messages from their parents. These messages appeared to imply that they should not be happy (a joylessness message) or they felt unloved (a lovelessness message) or they thought they were going crazy (a no-mind message). They were often depressed, found difficulty in coping with their lives and felt out of control. Years later, in the eighties, I discovered Steiner's work [55] on scripting in which he reported on 'No Joy, No Mind, No Love' life messages.

As a counsellor, one of the most difficult aspects of my work is working with depressives. It is very difficult to 'shift' some clients. By looking at their early messages they can make connections between what was said to them as children and how this is continuing to affect their lives in a negative way. My experience is that many depressives also carried the same kind of 'Joylessness' messages shared by those people dependent on drugs.

Recently I counselled a man who had been labelled by his doctor as a manic depressive. He began to improve noticeably when we looked at his early messages and he made the connection with the way in which his mother (a joyless woman, prone to depression) would be constantly picking on both him and his father, only to realise that he was emulating his mother by doing the same thing to both his wife and children.

It was whilst working with women prisoners I first knowingly came into contact with lesbians. The closed environment means that many had lesbian relationships inside prison, although outside they were straight. Others said it was great to discover that they were lesbians and how much better their sex lives now were. I was not there in a counselling capacity as I did not have the knowledge or the skills to support them but was told stories of their sexuality. Years later when working with other homosexuals, I found that when they explored their sexual messages there was a common theme in that they had been given directly or indirectly, verbally or non-verbally a 'wrong sex' message. For instance, statements cropped up like 'we really wanted a boy/girl when we had you'. This is not for one minute to say that this would be the only reason for homosexuality as, like gender, there has been a lot of research in this area. There are no clear-cut reasons for the apparent rise in so many homosexual people coming out today unless people are now being given tacit permission to pursue their preferred orientation. I recalled my conversations with the prisoners, when some homosexuals talked of their enforced sexual lifestyles in closed institutions, or declared that they had always felt a sexual attraction to their own gender.

Having observed the commonality of messages among addicts, – some women, some men, homosexuals, and depressives – I then considered the possibility that early sexual messages may be one of the numerous reasons for the diversity in managers' behaviour. Sexual messages may have some connection with their attitudes towards the opposite or the same sex and influence the use or misuse of their sexuality. It was because of my background as a management trainer, senior manager and counsellor, that I studied managers' sexuality at work. By looking at their sexual attitudes and listening to their sexual stories about themselves, others and the organization, I tried to analyse the ways in which they perceived that they were affected by their sexuality at work. Because of my experiences for a short time working in a prison and a long time in further and higher education I chose managers from these two different organizations, one open and one closed. Having completed the initial research I then went outside these areas and tested my findings in the public sector, industry, commerce and in medical settings. As a trained counsellor I recognised that for a researcher to explore the sensitive area of sexuality I would need effective counselling skills and an ethical framework in which to operate. I was confident that I had these qualities. Seven years later I now appreciate the difficulties of researching into sexuality at work, let alone convincing examiners of its value and importance.

My work experience made me aware of how people's sexuality may affect them at work, both negatively and positively. I found that some individuals were unable to break free from their early formed sexual attitudes, which were manifested in later life, while others benefited if they were able to explore their sexual attitudes and change them if they were destructive or disabling. However, I may only have been involved with people who had found that their sexuality created stressful situations for them, or possibly I had some responsibility for the way people explored their sexuality through the empathic attitude that I was emitting.

Having given the motives for writing the book I will now outline the format of the research. I will then go on to say what is meant by sexuality and look at what has been written previously about sexuality in the workplace.

An introduction to my research

This research explores the extent to which sexual attitudes affect behaviour in organizations and tries to establish the origin of those attitudes. Various organizations were chosen for the study in the UK and Europe and senior managers from both open (eg industry and commerce) and closed (eg the prison service) organizations were chosen for interview.

The study highlights how early sexual messages given to children can be recalled and how in many cases these messages continue to influence people as adults in organizations. The research addresses the way in which managers are affected by their sexuality at work and demonstrates that sexuality does affect the vast majority of managers at work to a greater or lesser degree. It begins by showing what is meant by sexuality (Chapter 2). Then it draws attention to the lack of previous qualitative studies and the need for further research in this daunting area of sexuality at work in organizations (Chapter 3). Then the research findings are presented in three ways.

Early sexual messages and experiences (Chapter 4)

Early sexual attitudes are explored and categorised and then it is identified whether the subject's attitudes towards sexuality have changed since their early years or whether these attitudes create inner conflict.

Managers' perceptions about sexuality at work (Chapter 5)

Managers reveal how their sexuality affects them at work, in interviews, meetings, promotions and relationships. These categories, among others, emerged through empathic interviewing and were supported by perceived organizational messages and stories. Many sexual experiences were shared by both men and women managers but others were only experienced by one gender.

Case studies (Chapter 6)

In this chapter I offer ten individual case studies that enrich the overall study. Some illustrations are given of how early sexual messages may affect managers at work, how sexuality may affect decisions at interviews and how sexual feelings or early experiences are projected onto other staff. I also show how sexuality affects relationships between staff or customers, how managers will promote staff because they are sexually involved with them and how they will appoint people to the organization because they are sexually attractive. Furthermore, I highlight how some managers' sexual orientation is either kept confidential or in actual fact is an asset to their work and promotion, whilst others have a fear of reprisals. Other stories show how confidentiality can be affected by sexual liaisons at work.

CHAPTER 2

WHAT IS SEXUALITY?

Sexuality has many meanings and is perceived by many authors to mean different things, but although there are numerous perceptions of sexuality, there is one certain fact: people's sexuality affects them at work. This can be demonstrated in how they think, feel or behave. I shall now explore what is meant by sexuality, demonstrate the diversity of the meanings of such an emotive word, and offer my own understanding of the term. Searching for previous writings on what is meant by sexuality at work was difficult because so little had been written. However, a great deal has been written about sexuality. The meanings are indeed wide and varied. Many authors have made pleas for research into this area of sexuality and I will suggest possible reasons why so many researchers and organizations may have avoided the topic.

Sexuality is defined in so many different ways that it is difficult to find any aspect of life that is excluded from such a powerful force, as can be seen from the following excerpts from literature. These definitions include various aspects of sexuality including gender, historical, private, attractiveness, activity, romance, threatening, stereotyping, biological, physiological, psychological, fantasy, power and political. Sexuality is diverse and can mean sexual orientation, sexual intercourse, sexual behaviour, sexual activity, sexual desires, sexual identities, sexual practices, sexual violence, sexual harassment, sexual fantasies, sexual experience(s), sexual domination, sexual abuse, sexual dynamics, sexual politics, sexual games and sexual discrimination.

This is supported by Keller [49] who believes that...

Gender and sexuality do not exist in isolation, but in their specific conjunctures with such divisions as age, ethnicity, class and bodily facility. The relationships of sexuality and sex, and gender and sex, are problematic...

Sexuality and gender become intensely bound up with history and politics. Our concepts of gender and sexuality, in terms of both of their social meaning and of the particular forms of their relationship, are determinedly historical. Thus, for example, what counts as 'sexual' in one historical period may vary from what counts as such in the next. In western society, and especially the Judaeo-Christian tradition, an enormous historical weight of religious, moral and intellectual opinion has accumulated against sexuality. Sexuality has historically come to be seen as something frightening, uncontrollable, illegitimate, unpredictable, chaotic.

Fear of sexuality has interwoven with men's fear and hatred of women and women's sexuality, and men's association of women with the dangerousness of sexuality.
Burrell [4]

Hearn et al. [6] found that during the time of their research, they had to broaden their definition of sexuality in at least two ways: firstly, they needed to see sexuality as an ordinary and frequent public process rather than an extraordinary and predominantly private process; and secondly, that sexuality was a part of an all-pervasive body politic rather than as a separate and discrete set of practices. So the term sexuality is used here specifically to refer to the expression of sexual or social relations, to physical or bodily desires, real or imagined, by or for others or for oneself. Others can mean people of the same or opposite sex. In contradiction, Stone [7] offers a different aspect of sexuality. . .

> *Despite appearances, human sex takes place mostly in the head, imagined or fantasised, sexual relations may be as important a part of sexuality as actual sexual practices. Sexual practices may range from mild flirtation to sexual acts, perhaps with orgasm, even with enclosure and/or penetration. Such acts may be accomplished willingly, unwillingly or forcibly by those involved.*

The phrase 'to be experienced' forcibly leads us on to the aspect of sexual power and politics. Sexuality is always political and usually involves power. This is visible in the abuse of power which can be seen in harassment, assault, rape, pornography and paedophilia.
But as well as the power and politics of sexuality there are also the different sexual orientations of sexuality:

> *it is important to emphasise that sexuality includes narcissistic, bisexual, homosexual and heterosexual preferences and practices and it also includes fantasy.*
> **Rich [8]**

My research would add 'autosexual' to these preferences. That is sexual gratification without the presence of another person.

It is the concept that sexuality is something that is private, which can make research into such an area so difficult. Sexuality has historically included privacy as a large factor in the many discussions or debates. Whilst the media now offer documentaries, phone-ins and chat shows on all aspects of sexuality, there is still a privacy about what most people do together.

Trying to define sexuality is difficult as it is surrounded by myths, stories and taboos and ranges through the psychological, physical, social, romantic, political and biological aspects of knowledge and experience.

Other definitions of sexuality given by different authors demonstrate yet again the wide variety of perceptions of sexuality, from romance to harassment. Dickson [10] defines sexuality as being that of sexual attraction which leads to the possibility of sexual activity, whereas Zetterberg [11] considers sexuality as romantic relationships; Harrison and Lee [12] refer to sexuality as sexual liaisons; Burrell [13] regards sexuality as a form of threat; and Kanter [15] only considers the element of sexuality as harassment. Hochschild [16], in her studies on air hostesses, offers the suggestion that sexuality is profitable since the management benefit financially from advertising female air hostesses as 'sexual' attendants to the passengers. The passengers are usually men.

One starting point in the consideration of the status and relevance of biological explanations of sexuality is that of Rubin [17] who has critically recognised the power of 'sexual essentialism – the idea that sex is a natural force that exists prior to social life and shapes institutions'. She states that...

The dominance of the thinking in folk wisdom has been reinforced through much recent theory and practice of medicine, psychiatry, psychology and the academic study of sex. These fields classify sex as a property of individuals. It may reside in their hormones or their psyches. In other words it may be construed as physiological or psychological.

WHAT IS SEXUALITY?

The idea that sexuality is about personal and political issues is endorsed by Brake [18].

> *The nature of sexuality is a subject which ranges into the difficult area of the personal and political. Sexual passion is the one area where the trappings of respectability and success have been thrown away for pleasure.*

Sexuality is wide ranging and its definitions – encompassing fantasy, practice, sexual orientation, infantile influences, relationships and behaviour – have social repercussions. Sexuality is no one thing: it includes and refers to the body and the sense of touch, emotion and desire, thought and fantasy, image and appearance. To reduce this broad range of powers, actions, thoughts and feelings just to sexual acts gives an inaccurate, even sexist view, of sexual realities. Sexist, in that some of the meanings of sexuality are given as stereotyping [14], harassment of women [15] – the majority of the authors are male, offering a masculine interpretation, although it should be noted that the male authors referred to in this section are eager to develop and try to demonstrate an empathic insight into the way women act or feel, pointing out possible events and situations that may contribute to the imbalance of sexual power, and the need for control of sexuality in organizations.

Some of the definitions covered in this review contradict each other, as might be expected. So it is necessary is to develop a broader definition and approach to sexuality in relation to how people think and feel, and if sexuality affects their organizational life, remembering that it is likely to mean a whole host of different things to the subjects interviewed. Having established that there were so many thoughts, feelings, definitions and areas of sexuality and that it may have any one of these meanings to the subjects, it was important to use this knowledge when interviewing my managers. When asked questions about how their sexuality affected them at work, some replied 'what do you mean by sexuality?' others 'can you define the word sexuality?' I would reply 'Whatever sexuality means to you'. By doing this, we moved on to their concept and understanding of the word 'sexuality' and what their issues were and what was important for them, rather than focusing on one specific, restrictive definition.

In researching sexuality at work I have taken account of the many definitions, and recognised that the personal and private aspects may mean that managers feel uncomfortable and anxious about disclosing fragments of their sexuality. Hence the need for confidential and empathic counselling skills. That sexuality is sometimes passionate enabled me to recognise many of the emotions surrounding interviews, whilst the psychodynamic element created an understanding of the intra-personal skills at play.

My approach covers the psychological, physiological and paedological aspects of sexuality by looking at remembered early childhood sexual experiences. Linking these to possible sexual attitude formation, attitude change and inner conflict between what is thought about sexuality and what is expected and appropriate behaviour, I recognise and show that sexuality is essentially about partnerships of varying orientations, with power related, profitable and political dimensions.

So the meaning of sexuality for me, in the context of my research, is whatever the individual thinks, believes, perceives or feels that it means to him or her. There are no right or wrong definitions from the interviewees. Some academics may disagree with this statement. In reviewing the numerous authors and showing the range of meanings offered, what then is the meaning of sexuality and where do I stand?

WHAT IS SEXUALITY?

My stance is that sexuality can be seen as any, all, or some of the following states:

>personal
>performing
>private
>psychodynamic
>persuasive
>psychological
>physiological
>pleasing
>penetrative
>placating
>paedological
>profitable
>powerful
>political
>perverted
>prostituted
>procreative
>partnering
>passionate

CHAPTER 3

WHAT HAS BEEN SAID ABOUT SEXUALITY AT WORK?

In answer to the above question – very little. I wonder why this is, especially as virtually everyone has experienced sexuality at work in both its senses. That is, sexuality working within the individual and between people, and secondly, sexuality in the workplace rather than in other settings.

As you can see from the previous chapter there are many authors who have contributed to defining sexuality but as to seeing how people's sexuality is experienced or exhibited at work, there is very little research or evidence. Many writers have made reference to the fact that there is an absence of research into sexuality at work. This neglect of such an important facet of working life is emphasised by the following authors [5, 10, 19, 20,]. Also, many authors have made pleas for research into the area of sexuality and I will suggest possible reasons why so many researchers and organizations have avoided the topic.

Despite the reluctance to undertake this kind of research, some studies have been carried out and I shall demonstrate some of the similarities and differences in the writings. Unfortunately these examples are quantitative studies rather than qualitative, and furthermore some are from 'pop' sources. Let us begin by looking at Burrell [4] who suggests that:

> *Sexuality is particularly under-researched and that the dominant paradigm, that organizations are patriarchal, will not be appropriately challenged until those most discriminated against can themselves research and theorise.*

As a woman I have persevered in my endeavour to research and theorise, hence this work which I hope will help partially to fill the theoretical gap. The omission of research evidence is now becoming more important because:

> *With the growing participation of women at all levels of the organization, trainers and researchers should be showing more concern for the issues of sexuality at work particularly to the management of attraction in the workplace. Organizations are a natural environment for the emergence of intimate relationships.* [20]

Among several women who have written on this topic Dickson [10] says:

> *In this compartmentalised society we assume we can keep work in the workplace and sex at home, so we are somehow faintly shocked when we stumble across the two linked together. And yet sexuality remains an implicit and powerful undercurrent in a lot of relationships which are explicitly professional.*

WHAT HAS BEEN SAID ABOUT SEXUALITY AT WORK?

Although some people may disagree and consider her work has been popularised, this common sense approach by Dickson is supported by Burrell [4]:

> *But while sexuality may be the most obvious element of gender relations in terms of common sense, phenomenology and everyday gossip it has remained the most unexamined within organization theory.*

The popularised work about sexuality is often denigrated by academics, but books written by authors such as Robin Skynner and John Cleese [21], Anne Dickson [10], as well as popular sex columns and agony columns in newspapers and magazines, may well have helped many people to handle their sexuality in a more enabling way.

Sexuality is private and organizations have no interest in managing people's private behaviour. Researchers appear also to have avoided stepping into such a pool of experiences and emotions. It is as though everybody at work leaves their emotions and sexuality at home, comes to work, works hard all day, goes home and picks up their sexuality and emotions there. You know this is not the case from your experiences at work. Many managers and staff will spend a disproportionate amount of their time dealing with people's emotions and sexuality at work. Resolving conflicts, avoiding certain individuals, appeasing staff who are complaining about intrigues getting in the way of their work.

Where do I stand? My aim is to bridge the gap between an academic piece of research work and a book that can be read by many, in the hope that some of my findings will help those readers to understand more fully how their sexuality may affect them or their colleagues. Let us now look at some possible reasons for the omission of research into sexuality in the workplace.

WHAT HAS BEEN SAID ABOUT SEXUALITY AT WORK?

What are the possible reasons for this lack of research into sexuality at work? Why is this area the most unexamined within organization theory? What reasons are offered for its exclusion, despite the pleas for more research? One reason may be that sexuality is difficult to handle and that it is a taboo subject. That men find difficulty in handling their sexuality is reported by Tom Boydell [58] who agrees with Burrell that:

Although sexuality is indeed a vital force, we don't really seem to have learned to handle it very well.

Whilst Boydell is referring to men, this may also be applicable to women. I agree that sexuality is regarded as a taboo subject by many managers, maybe through embarrassment or their own discomfort with sexuality. Burrell [13] adds another reason for sexuality being a taboo subject:

The Catholic Church focuses on the evils of sex and in doing so it effectively created strong sexual taboos.

This may lead to a denial of its existence and a reason for avoiding such research. This frequent denial of sexuality compounds the more general difficulties in studying sexuality. For example, the general problem of interpretation which pervades research into sexuality is of special significance in investigating the mixture of meanings within the sexual underlife of organizations. It is difficult to learn the truth from research findings which may be full of rumour, gossip, taboos, collusion, innuendoes and embarrassment. Whose truth are we hearing or seeing? Each individual has his or her own truth.

Sexuality remains hidden due to taboos that persist about it within organizations, along with the general taboos on the expression of personal feelings within organizational life. Although conversations in organizations may be personalised, the expression of personal feelings and particularly sexual feelings is more problematic.

Burrell [13], in answer to his own question 'why are sexual relationships not described or explained in the sociology of organizations?' argues that 'the exercise of control of sexuality is associated with resistance'. He gives evidence from institutions such as the navy and prisons that sex life is rife in the 'underlife' of organizations where it is apparently most controlled, but he offers no details on the managers. He does offer three explanations for the suppression of sexuality in organizations which might also account for the lack of research into it.

Firstly, the notions of civilisation and therefore of obscenity. I liken this to the Victorian idea of what was considered to be civilised and what obscene behaviour, which led to double standards. The civilised behaviour was being seen going to church, keeping up appearances and staying married, whilst the obscene behaviour would be the increase in prostitution and the keeping of mistresses. The fact that sexuality in organizations is widespread indicates to me that it should be explored, although it may be necessary to continue with the civilised behaviour of keeping up appearances within organizations.

Secondly, he refers to 'Religious morality and punishments for sexual activity' like Islamic stoning to death – a punishment for adultery. Researchers may not be stoned to death when studying sexuality; however, there can be a certain antagonism towards them as if they are committing adultery, or are being unfaithful to the organization by studying phenomena other than profit, products, systems or efficiency ratings, which are safer and more acceptable forms of research. The punishment aspect may be in dismissing the area and trivialising the work. Certainly my work was trivialised and laughed at because it created embarrassment for people who were or had been sexually involved with work colleagues.

Thirdly, 'Control over time and body by employers of labour' which is about value for money. If research into sexuality at work found that sexuality was taking up people's time by occupying their thinking, behaving or feeling, then such a situation would need to be addressed. For most managers this would be a difficult task. As Harrison & Lee [12] found when it came to responding to issues of sexuality 'the practice discovered from dealing with these sexual concerns was that most managers turned a blind eye'.

Another issue is that of the power of sexuality and the demonstration, especially by a woman, that sexuality is prevalent and powerful in the workplace, that it uses up people's psychic energy, affects people in meetings, at interviews and in their relationships with others at work. It would be prudent then to remove some of the power from many managers (many of whom are likely to be male). My findings now need to be addressed and turning a blind eye can no longer be an acceptable way of managing sexuality at work.

The attitude of the academic community which validates such work may also be relevant, since currently 'to teach about, indeed sometimes speak of, the sexuality of organizations is to invite the sarcasm, embarrassment and hostility of academic colleagues' [23]. For some it is not a legitimate area of study because of both the anxieties and the deep interest it often engenders in the audience (of academics in this case). A form of censorship is sometimes exercised as when, for example, Burrell [13] wrote a piece which made some reference to the existence in the Middle Ages of penalties for 'masturbation in church'. Strangely the editor of the relevant international journal removed this section because it would perhaps alienate 'Mid West accountants'. Funding bodies, too, are unlikely to regard the issue of sexuality in organizational contexts as being of paramount importance. The continued moves towards 'big science' with its associated features of a concentration of funding within so-called centres of excellence, the positive evaluation given to large research groupings and the process of placing it into hierarchies by peer assessment, point to a concentrated, centralised system of research. Sexuality is not high on the list of priorities advocated by institutional sources of finance. Much more emphasis is placed upon problems and improvements within the organization of production.

The knowledge that the research process affects the researcher and can produce negative emotions of anger or stress [26, 27] may be another reason why researchers avoid such a daunting area as you can see in the effects of this research on me, which are described in Chapter 7. Also the researcher has difficulty in trying to find literature and research on which to base their own inquiries.

To accomplish any worthwhile investigation into people's sexuality the researcher needs to be comfortable with their own sexuality (Perls [28]), have counselling skills which draw out evidence and be able to ethically handle the confidentiality of such private and often embarrassing revelations for both researcher and interviewee [29]

So, sexuality has been under-researched, with a few exceptions. Why should this be? Is it because sexuality combines all those issues mentioned earlier in meaning private, personal, passionate and therefore difficult to access? Is it because researchers are unskilled in interviewing on such an emotive area? Is it that people are anxious about their status and are fearful of skeletons in their cupboards? Is it the anxiety of confidential disclosures? Maybe it is the difficulty that many people have with their own sexuality that prohibits researching into the area, although this is opposite to what Bill Torbett [30] said, at a research conference on human inquiry: 'People research into what they are not very good at!'

Nevertheless, some research had been undertaken, but is of little direct relevance to my work e.g. Romantic Relationships [31], Managers and Lovers [32], Romance in the Workplace [33], Love at

WHAT HAS BEEN SAID ABOUT SEXUALITY AT WORK?

Work [12], Gender and Supervision[62] and Gender and Work [22]. These studies suggest that there is likely to be an increase in such relationships. They analyse the phenomenon with a mixture of liberal tolerance, an emphasis on non-harassment in love or sexual relationships and an unwarranted assumption of heterosexual norms. Whilst there may be a possible conflict in particular sexual relationships between men and women managers in organizations, doubts are expressed as to whether romance can be left to 'individual discretion, common sense or outmoded rules'.

The literature suggests that it is better 'not to mess about at work if you want to progress in the firm'; to turn a blind eye if you see anything going on; that sexuality may be painful and therefore may not be talked about; sexual involvement can jeopardise the firm's image; that there may be disruption to a relationship causing rivalry, jealousy and envy; that lovers can become preoccupied by day dreaming and their work may not be accomplished and the firm may be losing money in expensive phone bills; that there may be greater turnover of staff; that open sexuality may be embarrassing for the customers; there may be a breach of confidentiality which can affect the firm and individuals through 'pillow talk'; good staff may leave when they find the situation badly managed; male and female managers may be involved in sexual politics; and that sexual stereotyping may have detrimental effects on how managers are affected by their sexuality at work.

I agree that these are likely but I think that, on the other hand, there may be positive payoffs when people are sexually attracted to each other: they may be motivated to work more effectively and productivity may increase because of their sexual liaison; people may be motivated by the presence of the person to whom they are attracted or with whom they may be sexually involved.

Finally, I believe that I initially researched this area to build bridges between the sexes and to broaden men's and women's perspective on the opposite sex. However, since beginning my work on the subject my motives are now very much stronger and I feel that my research is now a challenge. This is mainly because of the effect that the research itself and some parts of the literature search has had on me, particularly the section which offers reasons for the omission. To summarise, my experience has been that these omissions occur because:

- of the possibility that studies in sexuality are not easily accepted by the academic community;

- the topic is difficult to handle because so much emotion is involved from both participant and researcher;

- sexuality is private, and it is difficult to pry into people's private lives;

- sex is a taboo subject and (some of the taboos may have stemmed from religion which can create barriers for both interviewer and interviewee);

- sexuality may be seen as obscene;

- the idea of morality and punishment may affect the researcher;

- of the fear that if individuals' sexuality at work is discovered they might lose their jobs or lose the respect of others;

- of the idea that if organizations are made aware of any research demonstrating the existence and effects of sexuality work on managers, they may have to address it and turning a blind eye will not be acceptable so findings are likely to be refuted.

WHAT HAS BEEN SAID ABOUT SEXUALITY AT WORK?

Sexuality in organizations

The meaning of sexuality is varied and diverse, so here I explore two aspects: the psychodynamics of sexuality and then the need for controlling sexuality in organizations.

Within the studies of group dynamics in organizations, attention is drawn to the importance of communication, bonding and role conflict. [34]

Though sexuality is not specifically mentioned in Argyle's work, the language of 'interpersonal attraction', 'sense of belonging', even 'isolation' and the 'socio-emotional' suggests that emotionality and sexuality are seen in de-sexualised 'structures' of the organization. The sexual psychodynamics of organizations has roots in the studies of intrapersonal as well as interpersonal skills, showing that emotions and sexuality affect work performance in organizations.

Recognising the effect of sexuality in organizations was greatly facilitated by the events of the Second World War...

a social process in which the kind of organization and discipline of the anal personality becomes dominant. In effect, this control institutionalises a redirection of sexual energies, repressing explicit genital sexuality while allowing and encouraging the expression of anal eroticism in sublimated form. This sublimated anal sexuality has provided much of the energy underlying the development of industrial society. [13]

The need to control sexuality is further emphasised by Burrell [13] as he offers the possibility that:

Sexual drives and fantasies shape corporate policy; neurotic behaviours

WHAT HAS BEEN SAID ABOUT SEXUALITY AT WORK?

shape compulsive, paranoiac, masochistic, and other enactments of the environment and work relations. A repressed sexuality underlies many of the most difficult and entrenched corporate problems.

If this is the case then as Hearn [6] suggests:

A full understanding of the significance of repressed sexuality thus leads us to a new kind of contingency theory of organization. Organizations are not just shaped by their environments; they are also shaped by the unconscious concerns of their members and the unconscious forces shaping the societies in which they exist.

If sexuality is not controlled then punishment appears to be required. Burrell [4] has identified writings which show that even in medieval monasteries, convents and churches, outrageous sexual behaviours presented a major problem. Manuscripts from the seventh and eighth centuries reveal that punishments for different classes of sexual misconduct were devised in elaborate detail. Some of the most extreme offences called for castration, while others required extensive penitence. Thus a monk found guilty of simple fornication with unmarried persons could expect to fast for a year on bread and water, while a nun could expect three to seven years of fasting, and a bishop 12 years. The punishment for masturbation in church was 40 days' fasting (60 days' psalm singing for monks and nuns), while a bishop caught fornicating with cattle could expect eight years' fasting for a first offence and ten years' fasting for each subsequent offence. Different organizational cultures use punishment for adultery like the stoning to death in Islamic countries already mentioned or removal of the neck bands from women in certain parts of Africa.

The aspect of controlling sexuality in organizations is endorsed by Jackall [35]. As his findings showed, 'you should never get your meat where you get your bread and butter', meaning one must not enter into any sexual liaisons that might jeopardise other important social relationships or one's public image. One does not therefore sleep with one's boss's secretary, and one should never, of course, allow oneself to become so infatuated with another person that one loses control.

This conjecture was formed from Jackall's core data of one 103 intensive self-structured interviews. There was one recurring sexual story about the male president of a company having an affair with one of the middle managers. The woman's husband was paid off in hush money. The interviewees who recounted this story, with one exception, had no moral qualms about their bosses' sexual behaviour as such. They felt that both were constantly under great stress, especially the President of the company and if he wanted 'a little honey on the side', who was going to say that he shouldn't have it? Nor did managers have any problems with the mysterious monies supposedly used to pay off the woman's husband.

Whilst no criticisms were made about the sexual liaison taking place, there was a conflicting view that all the managers criticised and condemned, without exception, both the President and his aide for being out of control, or for losing their cool, or for acting irrationally. Yet again there was the 'turn a blind eye' syndrome and this reaction also emphasises the importance for some men to be in control, so maintaining power. It is not so much the act but the ensuing controlling behaviour that is important in organizations.

I chose different organizations – open and closed – for my research. The open organizations included further and higher education, industry, commerce, public bodies and medical settings, closed organizations were represented by the prison service. Further and Higher education were chosen because most of my working life was in the field as described in Chapter 1; prisons for two reasons: my early experience of working in a closed organization at a women's prison where I first became aware of homosexual behaviour and, secondly, because of my later work with prison education officers on counselling and stress management courses for the Home Office. The managers in the prisons were not in a closed organization all the time so this categorising did not necessarily apply to them, but it did apply to the prisoners with whom they interacted. It is common sense to recognise that sexuality will be present in the interaction between men and women, men and men, women and women, whether they are in an open or a closed organization. Although initially I began work with 128 interviews in these two areas I later included other professions, making the sample 402 in all, to test out the viability of my earlier findings. Hence managers from industry, commerce, leisure industry and the public and medical sectors were interviewed.

Having discussed what has been said before about their sexuality at work, let us now consider what may influence the way in which managers are affected by it.

What influences the way in which managers are affected by their sexuality at work?

Just as there were many different concepts about sexuality, there are numerous influences on the way in which it affects managers at work. I am taking just one facet of a multifaceted subject, that is, early sexual messages. I wanted to see if managers still believe or carry these early attitudes; if they are still influenced by them or if they have changed them.

Do our childhood experiences affect us sexually as adults? Certainly present cases of abuse of children by parents, social and residential care workers and priests have indicated that the perpetrators were affected by their own childhood experiences. It is not only the behaviour that is experienced in childhood but also what we are told which affects our thinking and hence our behaviour. In Freudian terms the 'Id' is the childlike drive' Cooper [36] adds to this concept: 'The Id is the libido which is the sexual pleasure drive'. Adult sexuality in the large part stems from childhood experiences, internal conflicts and repressed instincts passed on to us as children. The family has a major impact on a person's sexuality and is the ultimate basis of our sexuality. So in what ways does the family have a major impact on sexuality and provide its ultimate basis?

To begin with, consider the model of transactional analysis. One author, Berne [37], offers a model which suggests that we have several ego states: parent, adult and child. The child is the Id to which Freud refers. Berne was a follower of Freud but thought that his language was very complicated so he devised a model that he wanted seven-year-olds to understand. One critique of this model is that the academics took hold of this concept and transformed it into a convoluted theory which is very suspect whilst other academics consider that transactional analysis is 'pop' psychology'. Nevertheless, I believe that there are certain aspects of sexuality that originate in childhood – in other words, what we are told as children about how sexuality may affect us as adults – unless of course we decide to change these messages. This is the idea of 'script analysis' according to Berne [38], that may influence our sexuality as adults.

What are scripts? Scripts can be given verbally or non-verbally. Sometimes people are unaware that they are carrying these messages, because they reside in the subconscious. At other times they may be consciously aware of them and adopt a particular script because of its 'payoff'. Turner [39, 40] offers the following explanation of scripts.

Our script conditions our lives. It is the basis on which we live out our days. It determines much of our behaviour, our images of ourselves and others, our dreams, ambitions and expectations. Our script is formed when we are very young. It is the process of being made from our birth up to the age of seven or eight. After that, though we may modify it in various ways, its main lines are set. We have by then come to some firm decisions about what we are like, what others are like, what life is all about, and what part we are going to play in it. Henceforth we

WHAT HAS BEEN SAID ABOUT SEXUALITY AT WORK?

are captive to our script and dutifully play out our role.

While I agree with the effect of scripts, I must emphasise the possibility of changing them. By becoming aware of those early messages it is possible to change your attitude or behaviour if you want to. This work was relevant to my study of how, or if, managers are affected by their sexuality at work. I asked subjects to recall their early childhood messages about sexuality and looked at whether these had changed or remained constant. The idea that scripts are constructed unconsciously poses difficulties on which I comment in my research methods (obtainable on request from the publisher). This model of scripting is limited because, of course, it is what is remembered, rather than what was actually said or done at the time. So as adults, managers may be able to remember their religious or other forms of attitude formation, and their early sexual experiences, but it is important to be cautious about such recollections. So one of the major influences that can affect how managers manage their sexuality at work is likely to be their early childhood messages.

A social psychologist's approach would be that it is likely that sexual attitudes, acquired as children, may influence how managers operate at work – attitudes being the social psychologist's central concept. We can begin to incorporate affective functioning, emotions and feelings into our portrait of the person as a processor of social information. Attitudes are likes and dislikes, affinities for and aversions to persons, groups, objects, situations and the environment. Social psychologists have studied attitudes as one component of a three-part system: cognitive, affective and behavioural [24].

Researching into this difficult area means that it is important to define sex role, sex typing and gender identity. In the field of research into sexuality it is important to understand an individual's own interpretation and clearly distinguish between sex roles, sex typing and gender identity. Sex role is best defined as referring to those behaviours understood or expected to characterise male and females within a society. Sex typing refers to the acquisition of characteristics and behaviour that a culture considers appropriate for each gender and develops through parents, peers and cultural influences [25]. Sex typing must be distinguished from gender identity which is the degree to which one regards oneself as female or male.

So what has been said about sexuality at work? That it is private and can't be seen, so researchers and managers can't see it is nonsense because it certainly can be seen in the media and in an organization, that is in the way people behave towards each other at work. The idea that organizations are a natural environment for relationships to develop is certainly evident in the number of people that meet at work and marry or set up life partnerships together, as well as those relationships that start and end with either positive or negative consequences.

Although little research has been done, popular columnists are seen to be dealing with all kinds of questions and requests for help with people's sexuality in organizations. There is no question that it exists unless all the letters and stories are fabricated, which I doubt. So let us begin to unravel some of the myths about sexuality and start by looking at people's early messages about it, what they were told and if they still believed some of those sayings.

CHAPTER 4

EARLY SEXUAL MESSAGES AND EXPERIENCES

Before reading on, complete the questionnaire so that you can check out if your own experiences are highlighted in the research. If you do it later you will be influenced by what follows.

Personal Questionnaire

Please write any stories or comments that you would like to, on the following suggestions:

1. The messages I was given (spoken or unspoken) when I was a child about sex and/or sexuality were:

2. Now, my attitude towards sex is:

3. My first sexual experience was:

EARLY SEXUAL MESSAGES AND EXPERIENCES

4. The sexual messages in my organization (workplace) are:

5. My story of sexuality at work is:

6. Other stories of sexuality at work that have happened are:

7. At work, my sexuality affects me in the following ways (or my sexuality does not affect me at work):

In order for me to analyse this sample study would you complete the following information. Please tick the correct or nearest descriptions. If you prefer not to mark the pages, then photocopy them. Thank you.

Gender   male [ ]   female [ ]

Age   20-35 [ ]   35-50 [ ]   over 50 [ ]

Marital status   Married [ ]   Living with partner [ ]

                     Single (living   Single (living with
                     alone) [ ]   relatives or friends [ ]

Job   [   ]

Geographical place   NW [ ]   NE [ ]   Midlands [ ]
of work   SE [ ]   SW [ ]   Scotland [ ]
                         Wales [ ]   Ireland [ ]

My sexuality affects   Frequently [ ]   To some degree [ ]
my working life   Not at all [ ]

EARLY SEXUAL MESSAGES AND EXPERIENCES

My sexual orientation is: Homosexual [ ] Bisexual [ ]
Heterosexual [ ] Autosexual [ ]

Introduction

This chapter shows how men and women managers were affected by their recalled sexual messages received as children. The material was gained from 126 in-depth interviews and 276 written personal documents. In total 402 people participated. Firstly I look at early recalled sexual messages and then consider whether the managers still carried these messages. Then I move on to explore managers' first sexual experiences. At the end of each section the findings which were shared by both genders and those experienced by each gender are shown. All these differences and similarities are drawn together and analysed at the end of Chapter 5.

Early sexual messages

Two aspects emerged and are addressed here. These concern attitudes and inner conflict. Firstly, early recalled childhood sexual messages remain strongly with men, whereas women are more likely to change their sexual messages and this is found to be typical in the following analysis. Secondly, men experienced more inner conflict through their sexual messages. This may be because they had not changed their attitudes – or maybe women felt more comfortable with me in the interview and thus were able to admit to changing. Perhaps the men were influenced by me as a woman researcher and still wanted to maintain their 'macho' image – or maybe the male stereotyping of men, i.e. not showing signs of weakness may have been around. It could be that as a researcher I am guilty of stereotyping men and women. It would appear that men and women will carry different sexual messages, but some are shared. So what were the sexual messages that men and women recalled, and from these messages what categories emerged? At least 50 similar comments would establish a category. From the first enquiry about early sexual experiences – 'What sexual messages were you given when you were young?' – the following patterns emerged.

Female managers

The categories which were only shared by the women managers were mainly concerned with the memory of marriage, having to endure sex and/or feeling embarrassed. Although sometimes I only produce a few examples in a category, they are similar to other similar statements. One of the strongest messages was one of 'Nice girls don't', but this was also given to men so it appears under the shared experiences of messages received.

Warning bells not necessarily wedding bells!
The greatest number of messages shared by the women managers were those referring to marriage. Over half of the women associated their sexual messages with marriage in some way and many of their recollections were remembered in a negative way.

'It was something men did to women in marriage' said Tina, a sentiment echoed by, 'From my mother it was something that was endured by women in marriage' grimaced Maureen. Two further conflicting memories of sex associated with marriage were expressed with 'Save yourself for marriage to keep respect', and 'Don't get pregnant before marriage' recalled Brenda. 'It was definitely tied up with marriage' said Rhona. 'Sex is no big deal, be careful, perhaps it's best inside marriage,' offered Mary, and from Margaret, 'It was a dirty and a forbidden thing outside marriage.' Gemma said 'Sex is rude and should not be talked about as it is only for husband and wife.' Further marriage messages were 'My mother hated marriage and tried to get me to dislike men.' 'Sex is only for marriage and for the procreation of children.' 'It is not nice but necessary for marriage and

EARLY SEXUAL MESSAGES AND EXPERIENCES

'Good girls don't. He won't respect you. It's up to the man to ask and the girl to say No. You must save it 'til you're married.'

Other comments included 'Keep it for marriage, a man knows if you've been with anyone else.' 'Sex in marriage is like petrol for the car.' 'Happy in bed is happy in marriage.' 'Get a ring on your finger before you let them touch you.' 'Men are only after one thing so get them to marry you first.'

The only positive memory that emerged associated with marriage was that recalled by Irene which brought a happy smile to her face. 'Both my parents said if you get pregnant, come home, we'll sort it out and there is no need to get married.' Nevertheless, she later said 'but thinking about it, there was a message of 'don't indulge in sex because it makes you pregnant and you don't want that before marriage.'

Sex is to be endured

This type of message was only recalled by women: the idea that sex 'is something to be endured within marriage' as Maureen recalled. Typically another comment was added to the marriage comment, that sex was a chore, a taboo. 'It was something men did to women in marriage.' Another woman had conflicting sexual messages in that from her mother she received the message that sex had to be endured but from her father 'sex is natural, have fun and enjoy it'. These messages appeared to give her the feeling that sex is something that is a duty, something that a woman needs to do for a man. It may also indicate a male power basis in their thinking. In addition, other comments were made like 'you have to put up with it; keep your man happy in the bedroom; never refuse a man his oats; they can turn nasty if you refuse it; get a nice home off them and you can put up with sex'.

EARLY SEXUAL MESSAGES AND EXPERIENCES

Sex is embarrassing – Be modest

The idea that sex or one's feelings or thoughts about sexuality cause embarrassment or require modesty, again was only expressed or experienced by women. Feeling embarrassed about one's sexuality was also a strong category. Some women still held strong associations with certain words or situations.

'I still get embarrassed when I see egg sandwiches!' How strange, you might think, but as the story was told, it was the association of egg sandwiches with being found out in a sexual incident as a child that created the embarrassment. The women in this category showed signs of embarrassment when being interviewed and when they associated their messages with their present sexual practice. This category also includes statements like; 'Puberty was a time to feel embarrassed about physical developments. I was rather ashamed about sex and was told that I should cover up,' said Rhona as she pulled her arms around her breasts. And Jennifer remembered, 'Anything is acceptable between consenting adults. But not to take place where it might embarrass others.' Jan later described how embarrassed she feels in meetings when sexual things are being discussed. She recalled the time, at a management meeting when they were discussing HIV and HIV safety. 'I could feel myself just going redder in the face. At my age you'd think I could manage a meeting better than that.'

Sonia spoke of how embarrassed she was made to feel about her genitalia:

I was told how rude I was as I touched myself and I must never do that because my fingers would drop off and everybody would know. I remember being so embarrassed by my body. I still don't like seeing the diagrams in the biology labs or the nude models in the art department. I avoid going anywhere near the section on a Thursday afternoon because that is when they have them in.

EARLY SEXUAL MESSAGES AND EXPERIENCES

'I remember', said Yvonne:

My mother told me that sex was rude and not enjoyable, though necessary, and that as a woman it is important to be modest, but from my father I received the message that it was a little embarrassing but okay. Also I recalled another message from my cousins that it was okay to look at each other providing adults didn't find out!

She had received a mixture of messages from parents and peers (but later her attitude changed).

The passing down of attitudes towards marriage and sex roles between mothers and daughters is confirmed by Rollins and White [60]. In their research they looked at the role of the family in relation to the attitudes of mothers and daughters to sex roles. Having reviewed their evidence they found a significant correlation between the mothers' and daughters' attitudes towards marriage, children and careers, regardless of family types. Unfortunately they did not measure the fathers' attitude, as without this information the exact process of sex role attitude formation cannot be judged. This work also indicates the role of the father in the recalled messages. However, more importantly it indicates that women were more likely to change the attitudes received from either parent than were men.

Some of the women would begin by saying that sex wasn't talked about really but would go on to say that they still picked up messages. However, the male managers were more prone to say 'sex was never discussed.'

Male managers

The main early messages that male managers shared with each other included 'Big Boys Don't Cry,' 'Be a macho man' in no uncertain terms, to not showing feelings of grief by crying and many homophobic recollections. Many of their comments overlapped these categories. As with Tony who said 'I remember being told 'Don't start crying; you're a big strong man now and people will think you are a sissy poof boy if you cry''.

Big boys don't cry
This category was also strongly supported by the second highest percentage of men, who responded to the question with comments like 'Big Boys Don't Cry'. 'Always be brave, a man never cries.' 'It is sissy to cry.' Even the feminine members of our family 'stressed manliness to me' was a point made by Peter. The idea that big boys don't cry and don't show emotions was a heavy weight for many of the men to carry throughout life. The messages of 'Big Boys Don't Cry' caused a great deal of upset amongst the men. Parents appeared to have been trying to make big strong boys.

Macho men
The word 'macho' is used with great regularity in the Nineties and yet it was only used once as such in the messages reported. However, the implications of being a macho male were strongly reinforced within the male group. This message had been picked up sometimes through 'Big Boys Don't Cry' but also through such statements as 'You must be strong and brave because that's what girls like'. 'Always be brave and never cry.' 'Be manly.' One man wrote:

Boys = masculinity = virility = power = macho functions and expectations

Girls = femininity = weakness = subservient expectations

Homophobia
The idea that 'boys equals masculinity equals virility equals macho functions and expectations' was expressed by other men as they indicated the homophobic messages which had been relayed. These messages were more likely to have come from their fathers. One of the managers interviewed stated that he was bisexual, moving towards being heterosexual; other managers talked about their homosexuality. Of these one man said that he had lived with his partner for 25 years. This particular man started his recollection with the words 'With sex, I suppose I received neutral messages, I don't recall any strong messages. With sexuality, I was told the standard stereotypes; men should act as men, etc.' He then went on to talk about the negative messages of deviations: 'I had strong negative messages re deviation from heterosexuality.' The latter seems a pretty strong message to me. Also 'men as men' would probably be balanced with 'women should act as women', and, as he said, 'You don't mix the two!'

It would appear that he did 'deviate from heterosexuality' and did allow himself to show both masculine and feminine traits. Later in reply to 'Does your sexuality affect your work?', this same manager said 'I expect that I give off the right signals to show confidence, ability and competence. I show enough non-aggressive behaviour and anti-traditional hierarchies stuff to be attractive both to women and to men whom I wish to work with. I think I am an attractive personality. This must involve sexuality.'

Other homophobic messages were 'Be a normal man'; Don't turn out queer', 'Only fancy women'; 'Keep away from Nancy boys' and 'Make sure you don't hedge your bets.'

Messages shared by both sexes
Although the messages relating to men or women only were very strong and powerful in how they had been remembered and in many

cases also how they had been acted upon, there were in fact more messages that were shared between the sexes. These include the thought that sex was enjoyable but there were conditions attached. There were career implications, that sex was something that carried lots of warnings, beginning with 'It's wicked', 'Don't', that 'Nice girls don't', 'It is dirty', 'Women are supreme temptresses' and some initiated sex stereotyping. Also both men and women experienced the message that 'sex is something we don't talk about'. However, the strongest category in terms of the number of people who made reference to it was that *sex is something that is not talked about*. This came out in many different forms. Often individuals would begin with this but then go on to realise that there were other, maybe non-verbal, messages that they were picking up despite there being a lack of specific words.

Sex is enjoyable – BUT!
There were mixed messages received in this category. Brenda and Carol had mixed messages from their parents. Both had positive messages from their fathers. For example, Brenda remembered her father saying 'Sex is natural, have fun and enjoy it', but from her mother, 'Sex has to be endured; and Carol recalled her father saying 'It would be a lovely natural experience', but the mother said 'It's overrated'.

Meanwhile Keith recalled 'It is enjoyable and fun if treated responsibly' from his father, but went on to say that the messages were mixed because he also recalled the message from his mother that it was something embarrassing and unpleasant and naughty – to be ignored and hidden.

Few people mentioned the word 'love', though one man did say that he was told by his father that sex was enjoyable but it had to involve love. Lucy's addition was that sex was a really good thing but it was not physical; it was a state of mind. Her father's words still rang in her ears years later as she realised her marriage was only based on sex yet she wanted emotional intimacy as well.

Noticeably in all the cases quoted and in three-quarters of this category it was the male parent who passed down the positive attitudes, whilst it was the female parent who passed down the negative messages.

Career or children
Fewer men than women shared similar messages about the aspect of sex affecting their career because of dependents. The female point of view was that of 'You're a career girl. I'm amazed you want to have a child; you must choose between either job or children. You can't do both.' Meanwhile, the male version was encompassed in Philip's comment 'Be careful otherwise you'll have to get married, just like our inferior relations and then they, pretty women, will have ruined your career prospects!' This was probably referring to the fact that his studying would be interrupted, rather than that children would ruin his career. Philip later admitted that at work he had experienced several disabling relationships with women which had affected his career prospects. He was involved in sexual relationships at work and in one this resulted in a sexual harassment claim against him rather than his studying being interrupted.

However, the career or children implications were different for the women. It was that as a mother you are expected to look after your children first and any paid job is a secondary consideration.

As the age range of the managers were between 35 and 50 some of their parents were likely to be of the age when they were young, of remembering when women teachers had to leave their profession if they married and choices had to be made between career or children. This was so in the 1920s. Partington [41] explains how there was a high proportion of unmarried women in professions because of the 'local marriage bars on women', that is that married women were barred from teaching. When the managers were children, 35 to 50 years ago, there was also no legislation on maternity leave as there is today, so perhaps some of these comments reflected the society of their parents' youth. Though I doubt if the message that sexuality can affect your career is very different today, in the Nineties, even with all the new legislation that has taken place regarding maternity leave and equal opportunities, and the changes in patterns of employment. Today's young parents may have different stories and reasons for their 'career or children' choices but we will not know that for another generation.

Don't
There were many shared don'ts from both genders. Firstly the women reported 'Don't do it' from Kate; 'Don't get pregnant before marriage,' said Brenda; 'Never let a man touch you down there' grinned Irene; 'Nice girls don't, and anyway, if they do they don't enjoy it!' chanted Pat; 'Masturbation is a filthy, dirty habit and it makes you blind,' mimicked Barbara; 'I had an indirect sexual message which was generally to desist,' cogitated Carol; 'You are too young and good girls don't,' smiled Liz.

The men volunteered the following memories: 'Nice girls don't have anything to do with sex' from Arnold. A specific don't from Bill was: 'It was dirty and don't ask questions about it'; but there were many other don'ts implied, e.g. 'Don't talk about sex' was the message that Geoff had received, and 'Don't be homosexual' in 'Don't be feminine' was the memory that Roy had when he recalled 'I had strong negative messages about deviations from heterosexuality.' 'Don't do it, was also implied in 'masturbation is bad and wicked' from Ted. Graham had difficulty recalling his early messages but indirectly also shared a don't with 'My messages are not really that strong as I can't remember much about them. My mum told me not to come home to say I'd got a girl in trouble.'

EARLY SEXUAL MESSAGES AND EXPERIENCES

Sex is a wicked sin

Bob thought that his religion gave him a don't message. 'I remember that sex was very private and not something you talked about or alluded to within the family. My religion which was Catholicism gave me a very strong message about sexuality; it claimed that it was sinful, wrong and wicked.' Within the messages were some riders about religious sin and that sex was something for which people should be punished. Mary remembered how she was frightened by the sign 'God sees everything' in her bedroom. Her message was 'sex is a sin and to think it is to do it'. Whilst the majority of people thought that their early messages about sex came from their parents and some interviewees lived in residential homes, some early messages sometimes came from people other than the parents. One woman in this category said 'My religious upbringing made me think that sex was a wicked sin and I would go to hell if I did it. I know now that the nuns probably didn't say that as such, but I felt it.'

Men do this, women do that – Sex typing

As well as the stereotyping that occurred in some of the previous categories there were other specific messages and words that created the stereotyping of sex roles. These overlapped with the macho man category as in the case of Derek, who recalled that his messages came from the different words or stereotypes given to boys and girls. For boys, he remembered the words 'masculinity, virility, power, macho functions' and for the girls, 'femininity, weakness and subservient expectations'. This was echoed by male comments of 'Boys play with trains, girls with dolls', 'Girls have to be looked after – they cry if they are hurt'. 'Boys are strong and girls look after you.'

Female managers were told 'men are more active and more responsible'. 'Men need looking after to be able to keep you' and 'Always keep yourself attractive and sexy for your man because otherwise he might go off with someone else'.

EARLY SEXUAL MESSAGES AND EXPERIENCES

Throughout the interviews odd little sayings, philosophies, platitudes or prophesies would pop out suggesting sex stereotyping, for instance 'If there were no bad women there would be no bad men' and 'Girls should be treated like china dolls.' These were still prevalent in the managers' stories about their sexuality at work.

The supreme temptress
That women were supreme temptresses was a further category shared by both genders. The women managers recalled messages like 'Get your man by keeping yourself attractive and sexy'. Alongside the supreme temptress message was the warning that sex is uncontrollable and secret. A message which remained very strong for Moira was 'If there were no bad women there would be no bad men.' Male managers offered 'Women will corrupt you', 'Beware of females; they use you', 'Women want a meal ticket', 'Girls get themselves pregnant to catch you', 'Never trust a woman. They tempt you with sex to trap you.'

Sex is something not talked about
Women shared the message of 'Not discussed' with recollections that sex was never discussed, something not spoken about, not to be mentioned: 'Sex was not to be talked about'; 'I don't remember the word ever being uttered'; 'It was secret and mysterious'. Ann suggested that 'sex was never openly talked about but I remember thinking that it must be something dirty and was what other people did, not us. It was only when I started my periods that my mother said anything at all about sexuality and that was "You'll have to be careful now 'cos you could get pregnant".'

One of the reasons for selecting and creating an age band in this study, 35 to 50 years, was in order to try to avoid too much bias with regard to different generation influences. These findings need to be read with that in mind. Some of the managers would be receiving their sexual messages during or after the Second World War and all of the managers would have received their sexual messages before the availability of the female contraceptive pill and the Sixties era of 'flower power'.

A greater percentage of men recalled sex never having been discussed, more so than any other identified category. 'Something that was not discussed,' said Don. 'The subject of sex was never brought up,' agreed Arnold, but he did add that 'Nice girls did not have anything to do with sex and girls should be treated like china dolls'. This idea is later developed in his management style, when he describes some sexual stories at work.

The fact that sex was not discussed was strongly supported by other men with comments such as, 'we didn't talk about it'. I went to a boy's school and the messages I received from my parents were 'We don't talk about this at home, but when you are of age, you'll find you know what you need to. But don't mention that in this house,' yet 'you're not a man if you don't do it' were the contradictory messages from his peers.

'I felt 'out of it' because my first sexual experience was very late. I was extremely shy and gave out messages that I did not want to talk about it' said one man, whilst other men added they were told 'not to ask questions about it' and 'that it was secret, hidden, something that caused sniggering, something that adults kept from you. 'However, when I fell on a post and it grazed my groin, my mother told me I must be careful about that area because I'd need it later on,' smiled Colin.

The memory that sex was something that was never spoken about appears to leave people with an attitude that sex is something not to be discussed in the family or elsewhere. As the research moves on you can see how the majority of men did not change their early messages, although a minority did. The men who retained their negative sexual messages often found it difficult to relate to or feel comfortable with women in the workplace.

Analysis of sexual messages

The early messages that were recalled fell into three categories, those which had been experienced only by women, only by men or that were shared. The patterns that emerged showed that the most commonly experienced messages for the women were those associating sexuality with marriage, whereas the strongest pattern that emerged from the men was that 'Big Boys Don't Cry'.

The messages shared by both genders were in the main: 'sex is something not talked about'. Sexual warnings appeared such as 'it's enjoyable – but', 'don't' or 'sex will spoil your career,' or they offered restrictive heterosexual sex roles which in themselves were warnings of 'unless you behave like this you will not be a fully developed or "proper" man or woman'. The following table illustrates the messages shared and split between the genders. There were many more shared early sexual messages than those associated with only one gender. It would appear that men and women have far more in common in terms of early messages than was anticipated. Certainly I was surprised at the findings.

Table 1. Analysis of sexual messages

WOMEN	SHARED	MEN
Sex is for marriage – so wait	Sex is not talked about	Big boys don't cry
Sex has to be endured	Sex is wicked – religious warnings	Be a macho man
Sex is embarrassing – be modest	Women are supreme temptresses	Don't deviate – be heterosexual (homophobic messages)
	Sex is enjoyable – BUT	
	Sex can ruin your career	
	Don't do it	
	Girls do this; boys do that (sex typing and sex roles)	

Attitude change: do managers still carry their early sexual messages?

Having noted the most commonly shared categories of sexual messages, now let us look at whether or not the managers' attitudes about sexuality had changed.

As stated, the pattern that emerged was that more women than men in the survey had altered their thinking on sexuality. Although a large number of the respondents said that their attitudes had changed, it can be seen later that many of the stories about their organizations still showed the signs of their early messages in the way they viewed the men and women around them. Cross references are made to this fact in the later analysis of sexual stories and organizational messages (see Chapter 5).

The following are examples of positive changes which enabled people to have a fuller and more enriched life, although some readers may disagree with the reports.

Women managers

'Don't do it. Decide whether you want a job or children' changed to 'I'm now much more relaxed. When I feel sexy that's fine; when I don't, that's fine also' Kate smiled serenely. 'If there were no bad women there'd be no bad men' changed to 'Something I do because I think my husband likes it and I now accept that occasional masturbation is a means of obtaining relief from tension.' Ann was happy with this shift.

A non-existent message changed from 'Cautious because of HIV,' and 'Nice girls don't' to a belief that women have as much right as men to have as many sexual partners as they wish.

'Sex is a chore and is something that men do to women in marriage and it is a taboo' changed to 'It is a natural physical and emotional function and is very enjoyable and brings me close to my partner. Sex is something I enjoy' – this was Tina's preferred state. 'Sex is to be endured' the message from mother, and 'Sex is natural, have fun and enjoy it' from father changed to 'Now I think that sex is open and honest. I have no problems about having discussions with my own family who are now 18 and 20 years old. They are happy to approach me with questions, but I am cautious about sexually transmitted diseases,' added Brenda.

'Desist from sex as it is tied up with marriage,' and 'puberty is a time to feel embarrassment and rather ashamed, and you should cover up' changed to 'As long as both partners are happy with all activities, nothing is wrong,' Rhona enthused. 'Nice girls don't and anyway, if they do they don't enjoy it' and 'masturbation is a filthy dirty habit and it makes you blind' changed to 'It gets better with age and experience and it's very enjoyable. What a shame I was so inhibited when I was younger,' Pat added sadly. 'It was something women endured within marriage' changed to 'Sex is a thoroughly enjoyable pastime within a warm loving relationship. I have a feeling of sorrow for my mother who couldn't feel the freedom to enjoy it,' Maureen added as she reflected on what she had just said. 'Sex is done behind closed doors and I would be told about it when the time was right' changed to 'Anything is acceptable between consenting adults.' 'But not to take place where it might embarrass others', 'You are too young and good girls don't' changed to 'It is joyful and can be great fun'; 'It was unmentionable, therefore not quite nice' changed to 'It's quite nice really'. 'It was a dirty and forbidden thing outside marriage' changed to 'It is a blessing. But I still feel too inhibited to enjoy sex fully.'

The majority of the women had changed their messages to something more positive than they had received as children. However, a few still felt that they had not really changed their attitude. An example follows from one woman who reported on how her conflicting messages had affected her.

'My father said that sex would be a lovely natural experience.' But her memory of her step-mother was:

EARLY SEXUAL MESSAGES AND EXPERIENCES

I remember she formally read to me from a book which was afterwards taken to her room. So sex was formal and was about information. My sexuality was played down by my loving father. I suppose because of my mother dying when I was seven, he was extremely frightened and protective towards me. I didn't go out until I was 18, just before I went to train as a teacher at training college.

She admits that now she holds the attitude that:

My body is insignificant and of no sexual interest to men. The last thing I would do is to flag a car down – that would mean showing a leg. I'm embarrassed about wearing pretty lingerie which could be construed as seductive. I love lingerie for its prettiness not for its provocativeness. I cannot watch love making on television; I feel very uneasy. Strange thing is I love intimacy, being touched and loved but have difficulty showing it sexually.

It can be seen from this that the idea that her 'sexuality was played down by my loving father' may still be around in her present attitude. Certainly later she adds that she uses her femininity at work, not her sexuality. She states that she prefers working with men because using her femininity gives her more power.

Male managers

The messages that men changed to reflect a more positive attitude towards sexuality follow. It is very noticeable that there were far fewer examples in this category than there were for the women. A sample of some of the messages that had changed include Don's 'It was dirty' altered to 'Now I'm much more open about my sexuality'.

'No messages were given to me. I discovered it (sex) in the third and fourth form at school, which was as all boys schools', but this changed also to now being 'open and honest', smiled Ted.

EARLY SEXUAL MESSAGES AND EXPERIENCES

'Boys should show their masculinity, virility, power, be macho, whilst girls should show femininity, weakness, have lower expectations' changed to 'The role of women has changed. Power has to be shared on the basis of equality. Sex is not to be feared', remarked Derek. This example correlates to sex typing in Chapter 2. That 'it was secret, hidden, something that caused sniggering, something that adults kept from you' changed to 'It is something for the daylight, for the moonlight; it is an integral part of life and it's a pity it has been identified as something separate with its own word', thought Colin. Even though Colin's attitude had appeared to have changed, later he used the word 'sniggering' when telling his sexual story about the principal.

'My messages are not really that strong as I can't remember much about them. My mum told me not to come home to say I'd got a girl in trouble.' This changed to 'when it happens it's wonderful, but I don't get hung up on it'. Graham offered. Gordon's mixed messages of 'Don't mention that in this house' from his parents and 'you're not a man if you don't do it' from his peers were now 'I love it. I believe it's OK outside marriage and inside it but it must be at least semi-love or very strong caring'.

Alan stated that he had changed his attitude but this had been brought about by the advent of HIV. His early recalled messages were 'not direct, but I was left to explore sex and sexuality for myself. However, there was an understood norm of equality on all issues surrounding sex, sexuality and religion.' Alan stated that this had now changed to, 'Sex is now somewhat different from my exploration years. I am influenced now by the advent of HIV which makes me value my free exploration in my youth which was untainted by any threat'.

The statements made by the men that showed that they had not really changed their attitudes from their early sexual messages included: 'Something important, but not overwhelmingly so.

Something that is most appropriate within marriage' was Tony's early message and now he agreed that his attitude was still much the same. He said 'I see all the damage and problems caused by people abusing sex and marriage that I suppose it is balanced by the good relations and stability achieved by those people that don't.'

Guy's early messages didn't really change, they were more of a self-fulfilling prophesy. Guy had been told 'We don't talk about it in this home, but when you are of age, you'll find that you know what you need to,' yet now his attitude was 'Find the right chemistry and you'll achieve nirvana.'

Experiencing conflict

Whilst many of the attitudes had changed from early childhood messages, many were still tainted by them. Some managers still carried some conflict within themselves about their present attitudes towards sexuality. There were more men than women in this category (see Table 2). This can be seen from the following statements. Two of the responses from the women were:

'My attitude has never been that men were more active and more responsible than women and therefore I found myself in conflict with others during my childhood, but my attitude to my sexuality and to sex is now positive,' celebrated Lynn. 'It isn't the only thing in life, as there is more to a relationship than sex. In fact it can be a block in working relationships,' Irene considered. 'I now believe that sex is fun, though I recognise that the messages I received when I was young do still inhibit my enjoyment and spontaneity of sex,' Barbara reluctantly admitted.

Meanwhile the responses from the men who were still in conflict with their early childhood scripts included such statements as 'Sex was very private and not something you talked about or alluded to with the family. My religion, Catholicism, claimed it was sinful and wrong' (Burrell 1989), but now this man added, 'My attitude is that it is not sinful or wrong, but it is very powerful and potentially destructive, especially amongst adolescents'. So there had been some change but the subject was still left feeling in conflict about what he was observing at work (later discussed) and what he now believed: that sex was powerful and potentially destructive.

Further examples are given that showed that the men's sexual attitudes affected their behaviour and created inner conflict. 'I'm still fairly repressed', said Geoff. 'It is enjoyable and fun, if treated responsibly', emphasised Keith. 'I'm not bothered by sex particularly – that is, regular intercourse. I am much more interested in more subtle sexual interaction between people. I don't think I'm scared of sex but I'm unwilling to upturn my life by inviting sexual attraction,' established Roy. An irrational emotive jump here from not being scared of sex to thinking that life must be upturned by inviting sexual attraction. Perls [28] theory is that reversal of statements helps people to come to terms with some of the denial. So instead of saying 'I don't think,' Roy needs to say 'I do think I'm scared of sex' and then see how that feels.

'…something which happens at home and is private. I do not talk about it,' Brian spoke quietly. His attitude had not changed from 'sex is something that is not discussed'. 'As long as there is consent between people it is no-one's business what they do. The state should stay out of people's bedrooms,' dictated Philip. 'Sex is fun. Romance needs sex to "fuel" it. Sex is part of an adult relationship between the sexes but nice girls are boring for an involved relationship,' mused Arnold who had received an early childhood message of 'Nice girls do not have anything to do with sex.' In order for Arnold to come to terms with his cognitive dissonance he had changed this to 'Nice girls are boring'.

'I am tolerant now and I have many friends of many sexual persuasions, but I found it hard to accept physical contact from men, even of my sons.' Peter's message had been that a man must 'always be brave; must be a man and never cry', even his female family members stressed how important it was for him to be manly. His message of 'always be a man' appears to have left him with a concern about being what is usually referred to as feminine when showing feelings. Perhaps his feminine stereotyping of women is that they touch and show affection to children but men don't, or maybe he is anxious about allowing the feminine side of himself to appear in case he loses some of his manliness.

Analysis of changing attitudes

The data supports the idea that many more women than men changed their early sexual messages to different attitudes and beliefs: this might be because women are more likely to share their feelings with other women, or it may be that women are more able to show their feelings. Maybe more women than men are likely to talk about their sexuality and their ideas may not be bound up with sexual images like being 'macho' or 'stud-like'.

Whilst lots of men and women experienced conflict in their sexual attitudes, a larger number of men than women experienced conflict with their present sexual attitudes. This strongly supports the theory that unless attitudes are changed to accommodate new behaviour then there will be conflict. This in turn supports the first part of the focus of the research that what managers are told about sexuality in their early childhood, forms certain attitudes and that men are less likely to change their attitudes and possibly may experience inner conflict because of this factor. Women, on the other hand, are more likely to change their early sexual attitudes and as a result do not experience so much inner conflict.

'Once the course is clear, the individual chooses to want to grow better rather than regress' [42], meaning that when individuals have recognised their conflict consciously they then want to improve their situation rather than stay as they are or move backwards. Many of the managers interviewed felt they recognised the significance of these messages on their managerial lives once they identified their attitudes and they wanted to progress and work on themselves. This is strongly highlighted in 'Nick's' case study in Chapter 6.

Table 2 demonstrates that 80% of women changed their attitude from their early sexual scripts, whilst only 20% of men changed theirs. Also 80% of men experienced conflict with their sexuality at work compared with only 20% of women. Interestingly, although there would appear to be a strong correlation between these two findings for men, this was not total, i.e. some men who retained their early attitudes did not experience conflict and some who changed their early attitudes did.

Table 2. Attitude changes and conflict – differences between men and women

WOMEN	SHARED	MEN
More women (80%) experienced a change in attitude	Attitude change	Fewer men (20%) experienced a change in attitude
Fewer women (20%) experienced inner conflict	Experienced inner conflict	More men (80%) experienced conflict

First sexual experience

Asking people what their first sexual experience was may seem to have little to do with management but early experiences have influenced so many people's lives and attitudes, as will be seen later in how sexuality affects managers at work. This is a particularly difficult section of the research to analyse since I allowed people to recall whatever *they* perceived as their first sexual experience. The range of answers was wide but it did demonstrate the extent of the concept of sexual experience. The findings also showed which experiences were confined to women, which to men and which were shared.

The element of abuse was uncovered in many interviews. This was still upsetting for the subject and although some had had counselling, others were talking about it for the first time. Anyone who knows about abuse will recognise the effect that this can have on an individual throughout their life, let alone in their attitude towards the opposite or same sex as a manager of people. 'The self concept does not necessarily reflect reality.' [43] In this case people's concept of their first sexual experiences may not necessarily be the exact way the experience occurred. In terms of self-concept a person may be highly successful and resilient but still view him or herself as a failure. So many of the managers who may be seen as 'highly successful' in their job could still regard themselves as failures in terms of their sexuality or even as a failure in terms of themselves as managers.

For both genders age played a significant role when managers were recalling their first sexual experience. Amongst the women the recalled age ranged from four to 28 years. Amongst the men the recalled age ranged from five to 19 years.

The differing concepts of first sexual experiences recalled by the women included unaided orgasm, petting, full penetrative sex, marriage, abuse and rape. Whereas the men's early recalled experiences ranged from being excited by a mother's legs in wellington boots to full penetrative sex at 15. Within this range was the category of assault or abuse. This topic was very disturbing for some of the men who had only ever told one or two people and some had never talked about it before.

So the shared experiences were the categories of ageism, masturbation, assault and abuse and making links with childhood messages. Whilst the latter category and ageism were not necessarily related to the first sexual experience they were repeated so often that they warranted a mention as shared experience.

EARLY SEXUAL MESSAGES AND EXPERIENCES

The women

Within the group of women the majority of the responses fell into the categories of either petting or penetration (the word penetration was used to mean full [vaginal] intercourse, whereas some of the men used the word penetration to describe anal sex as well as vaginal sexual intercourse). The other categories alluded to were those of orgasm, abuse and/or rape. The word rape was only used by women, so although incidents of rape had occurred among the men, they used the term abuse to describe the experience.

Petting

Within these comments it can be seen that many of the women had a poor self-image. 'It is difficult to recall exactly what my first sexual experience was because boys and girls played together. Play grew into kissing games, then on to "You show me yours and I'll show you mine" and later between 14 and 18 I was petting in ever advancing stages. 'My first penetrative sex was at 19.' Rhona offered later 'I am so unsure of myself sexually. I feel inadequate in bed. People at work see me as so confident and together because of how I act but also because I was one of the youngest senior managers in the country. But underneath I'm so scared by most of the men around me.' Memories of first sexual experiences not being very positive were also recalled. 'My first sexual experience was at 15, behind the church with Randy Shandy, petting.' Kate smiled, then added, 'My first experience of penetrative sex was at 19 at university but it wasn't very good.'

Susie recalled her first experience as 'kissing and petting with boyfriends in the park or at the end of my road when I was between 12 and 16 years old. Everyone at work seems to think I'm sexy but I'm not. I've never had an orgasm yet. Can you believe that at my age (mid forties).' Her account of first experiencing penetrative sex was when 'I lost my virginity at 16 with a boyfriend I had had for a couple of years'. Also Carol said her first sexual experience was 'At college with my third boyfriend who was the college shark. Not surprising really, I thought it wouldn't matter as he said he'd marry me,' she paused, breathed heavily and added 'I can't believe how naive I was. . . Yes I can. I must have been the only girl on the campus who, thinking red was a pretty colour, made her own lampshade in red and put it in her window. My cheeks are the same colour as I think about it now!'

Pat's statement included petting and penetration but she had first thought about masturbation as her first sexual experience as she said 'Masturbation at the age of 11 then heavy petting at about 16 to 18 and my first penetrative experience on marriage at 22. No, wait. My first experience was petting in the boys' cloakroom at school.' Although some women recalled their experiences in detail, on being asked about her first sexual experience, Rhona answered with just one word 'awful', even though it was an open question that is not supposed to bring a one-word reply. However, she went on to tell the story and gave reasons for the awfulness. Sandra's experience meanwhile had been 'in a cellar petting with a fire cadet at a party. We just kissed and cuddled. More romantically later with a French teacher in Nice.'

Marriage

Marriage was associated with early sexual messages for many of the women, as can be seen at the beginning of this chapter. Probably as a result of that, numerous examples were offered in this category by women who associated their first sexual experience with marriage. 'Full sex at the age of 21 on marriage', Brenda offered. 'On my honeymoon', said Mary. 'Full experience at 28 before marriage but with the man I married,' Irene stated. This was also shared by Belinda who said, 'With my husband. He was my boyfriend since I was 16.' Also with her husband, was Monica's recollection, 'At the age of 20 when I was married' and 'My first penetrative experience was on marriage at 22,' shrugged Pat.

'With my present husband,' said Margaret. 'It was pleasant but not dramatic with my first husband, although he could not make it. He had a piece of skin that prevented him from having a full erection. It should have been seen to when he was a small boy. Lack of good sex broke up our marriage five years later although I loved him as a brother,' Veronica reminisced.

Orgasm

Amongst the women's responses a preoccupation with orgasm emerged. Reference was often made to magazine articles describing multiple orgasms which subsequently made the women feel inadequate or sexless. Not having an orgasm made them feel sexually unfulfilled or odd in some way.

Fortunately, Shere Hite's work [57] was an important report in 1976, although the personal attacks that followed her publicity of *The Hite Report* overshadowed the importance of her contribution to 20 years of sexual and cultural history. Her work followed Kaplan's [58] findings in 1974 which stated that 8-10% of the female population has never experienced an orgasm, while 90% of all women seem able to achieve orgasm by some means. Furthermore, less than half of these women reached an orgasm without clitoral stimulation. This gave the impression that clitoral stimulation was wrong, or not normal. It also placed women who did not achieve a vaginal orgasm outside the expected response and personal satisfaction group, creating a sense of abnormality in women.

So Hite asked the experts – that is, the women themselves – and analysed 3,000 anonymous questionnaires (from a distribution of 100,000). She conveyed the women's experience and found that most women orgasm through direct clitoral stimulation and very few through vaginal intercourse alone. This is an acceptable viewpoint today, but it was not the case when these women managers were young.

Sexual orgasm was referred to in different ways, having had an orgasm or still lacking the experience of one. Most often was the comment 'I've never had an orgasm' or 'not until I was 42' (or a certain age). Here I give examples of three women's experiences of orgasm. One mentioned 'An orgasm obtained with no physical stimulation when I was six, running to school. I was half afraid and half excited by the prospect of being late' and the other woman replied 'I pulled a hair out of my "naughty" – that was what I used to call it – the hair seemed very long as if it went right up. I expect it was my first orgasm. It was a lovely feeling. I used to search for long hairs after that but I never found another one.' The third example is 'With my cousin, we mutually explored each other. It was the first time I had an orgasm. I had suspected that I was homosexual but I knew for certain then. It was a natural event, unplanned and in love.'

Rape

The number of women who had been subjected to sexual abuse (one in four), appeared to be higher than would be expected on the basis of the national figures for Great Britain – one in six [59] – although these figures are varying as more research is being carried out in the area of child abuse. My findings were that one in four of the women had suffered abuse. This is a small sample which may explain the discrepancy; however, other women to whom I have spoken are not surprised by this. The pain and anguish that so many women recalled was the most disturbing part of the enquiry.

I now give some examples of the stories told in this category. 'I was sexually abused by the son of my mother's friend when I was about four. It only happened once and this is the first time I have told anyone about it', Barbara confided. 'My first sexual experience was sexual abuse over a long period of time by a close family friend

EARLY SEXUAL MESSAGES AND EXPERIENCES

which started at the age of 11.' Lynn was tearful as she recalled the incidents. She had not changed her painful experience into a painful memory as is suggested happens in therapy for such traumatic happenings and a transfer which I believe is necessary. I worked as a counsellor with Lynn on some of the feelings that had emerged for her in the interview. The interview stopped as it changed to a client/counsellor relationship.

Joan revealed her experience 'with an older man, who by today's standards molested me' but this statement moved out of the abuse category for me as she added 'but it was not against my will'. Maureen's memory was painful as she recalled 'My first experience of sex was rape. I was attacked in the street and indecently assaulted at the age of 14. It's a good job my first lover was older and understanding. If it hadn't been for him, I'm sure I would never have developed a feeling of my own sexual self-worth. It's a miracle I'm not screwed up about sex.'

It is good to see this outcome as this was the woman who had been told by her mother that sex was something that women endured, but by her father that it was good, and by her cousins that it was all right providing the adults didn't find out. This central comfortable feeling that she holds about her sexuality becomes apparent in the later sections on sexuality at work.

Whilst so many women revealed rape and abuse as having been their first sexual experience, only a few men confided that there had been abuse or assault in their lives. The ones that did disclose these experiences did not use the word 'rape'. The word 'rape' has only recently, in the late Nineties, been used with respect to men.

The men

Unlike the women, none of the men recalled marriage as a link with their first recalled sexual experience, which is not surprising, as so many of the women had been given early scripting of marriage associated with sexuality. Instead, most of the men answered briefly and all but 15 mentioned their age when answering. Some mentioned their inadequacy, whilst some mentioned assault. The strongest category for the men was masturbation.

Masturbation

Religious teaching appeared to have played a large part in the guilt associated with masturbation. 'I thought I was wicked because it's a sin,' said Roy. The jokes about going blind, having hairy palms and the thought that God could see you doing it all added to the men's inner conflict. This category was strongly supported by the greater percentage of men as being their first sexual experience. Bob recalled 'masturbation which caused great feelings of guilt. 'By the time of my first heterosexual contacts there was no guilt since I had rejected my religion.' Masturbation was often given as part of a series of other experiences and the age at which they occurred. 'At ten or 11 I experienced mutual masturbation amongst peers. At 11 to 15 I was doing genital touching to females and at 15 I had full sex camping at a jazz festival — it was great!' Peter laughed. 'Masturbation was my first experience, but then everybody did it at public school. I suppose all the jokes about public schools and queers are based on the fact that it actually happens,' philosophised Ray.

Discovering

Some men shared the memory of discovering their sexuality. Don remembered 'fumbling around trying to find out where things were, in my early teens'. Graham, meanwhile, answered 'realising something was happening which I was not controlling when watching something erotic on the TV. I was probably about 11 years old at the time.'

'Overwhelming because I had a geographically isolated childhood and went to a single-sex secondary school. When I discovered' the other sex it was very difficult to know how to handle the experience,' admitted Keith.

'When I was at college I can't think of anything that was of importance. I felt that maybe it was a reward, by the woman, of some kind,' Derek quietly informed me, his early scripting having been not to talk about it! 'I remember trying to discover where to put it. I thought it was in the front and was shocked to find it not there. My sister's doll was all wrong. Even though I had a sister I never saw her naked, probably because she was so much older than me,' Tom sighed.

Shared messages

Assault
Both male and female managers shared several early sexual experiences. One of these categories was assault as described by men, but may have come under the rape category. However, I have separated these two categories as 'rape' for women which was always an heterosexual attack. (Although some men did reveal being assaulted by women.)

For instance, Rikki recalled how he had been sexually assaulted by his mother.

> *Nobody ever thinks of little boys being interfered with by their mothers. It's always men with little girls, but I can tell you it's probably the worst thing that ever happened to me. I was so powerless. I thought it was what all mothers did at first. I went to my aunt's and touched her breasts like my mother used to get me to do. My aunt slapped me and told me I was 'a dirty little bugger'. It's difficult to remember now but I was very confused. I listen to women talking about rape and assault and they often say ' you can't know how it feels.' I've never admitted that I do know. I guess I felt the same as a little boy.*

EARLY SEXUAL MESSAGES AND EXPERIENCES

Roland said:

'When I was 15 a male attempted to assault me, otherwise when I was 19 which was when I first kissed my first girlfriend.'

Whilst being assaulted was an experience shared by both male and female managers, the women talked of being assaulted but this tended to mean that men or women 'tried it on'. The effect of being assaulted varied. One woman said 'I was nine or ten I often worked in surrounding fields. This older boy followed me. He was about 14-15. I suppose I was assaulted because out of curiosity I let him catch me up. He sat me down and touched me between my legs outside my knickers. I cried; he stopped. I ran away confused about what had happened and I never told anyone.'

Some men recalled being assaulted in public lavatories, in residential homes, by priests, scout leaders, care assistants, friends of the family, teachers and other boys. The assaults ranged from being touched and played with to attempted anal access, which was sometimes achieved. As for the women, some of the recollections became upsetting and occasionally counselling was needed.

Full penetrative sex
Both sexes shared full penetrative sex as being their first sexual experience. Some of the statements were about anal sex which tended to be associated with early abuse. Other references to anal sex were added by homosexuals. This is not to say that only male homosexuals recalled this, as some women also had experienced it. Some women did experience anal sex but few (three) referred to it as part of this study. So full penetrative sex was considered by many to be their first sexual experience, but caveats were added: 'My first experience of sex was on my honeymoon, but I had played about before and got more excited than doing the real thing.' Men offered

EARLY SEXUAL MESSAGES AND EXPERIENCES

the ages from 11 to 21 when they first experienced full penetrative sex, whilst women offered ages from 15 to 22.

Ageism

Some responses were purely objective and short but all but three included the age element. 'When I was 18', Geoff replied. 'When I was 11, I was seduced or educated by a precocious ten-year-old girl from around the corner,' Arnold revealed. 'At 15 breast touching and then numerous genital touching at about 17. I had full sex at 19,' mused Gordon. 'Age five or six petting with the girl next door.' 'When I was nearly 13, it was very pleasant; other experiences around that age were not so pleasant,' remembered Tony. . . 'with a beautiful Persian girl, it was only very tentative; but she made me aware of girls. I was about 17 years old.' Ted's eyes danced as he recalled the delightful experience.

Making links with childhood messages

Within many of the interviews (three-quarters) people made links between their present sexual attitudes or behaviour, and their childhood messages – that either they still carried them or that they had worked on trying to change them.

Derek, questioned me on the phrase 'first sexual experience,' saying 'it depends what you mean by sexual experience.' 'Whatever you think or feel it means,' was my reply. 'Well probably being born, but I do not claim to remember it.' He went on to say 'When I was five-ish I was excited by my mother's legs in wellington boots and at the same age I stared up my grandmother's skirts. At seven or eight-ish I cut a piece of bike tyre inner tube to fit over my penis. At about six-ish Pauline Bristowe took me to the railway siding to explore my body. My personal archetype is that I prefer women who make the running, and that's the same for me at work.' He added, 'I've only just realised this about Pauline Bristowe.' Derek was pleased at having made the connection.

EARLY SEXUAL MESSAGES AND EXPERIENCES

Both men and women were able to link earlier messages to present sexual behaviour at work, as can be seen from the in-depth interviews in the ten case studies in Chapter 6.

Table 3. Summary of first sexual experiences

WOMEN ONLY	SHARED	MEN ONLY
Petting	Ageism (larger number of men)	Discovering own sexuality and that of others
Marriage	Full penetration (vaginal or anal)	Self and mutual masturbation
Orgasm	Assault/abuse	
Rape	Making links with childhood messages	

So the early sexual messages were varied and wide ranging. Now let us go on to look at what happens at work for managers, if their sexuality affects them and if so, how.

CHAPTER 5

MANAGER'S PERCEPTIONS ABOUT SEXUALITY AT WORK

What is happening to men and women managers at work? What are the sexual messages that they hear? What are the sexual stories that are told? How do they perceive their own sexuality and that of others? Is gender an issue for some managers? Do managers knowingly use their sexuality at work? In what ways do they experience their sexuality – as an advantage or disadvantage? Which work settings are highlighted where sexuality does affect managers work? These and other questions are addressed in this chapter which looks at how managers consider that their sexuality does affect them at work.

What are the sexual messages heard at work?
There were an enormous variety of responses to this aspect of the inquiry. One strong category emerged, which was that of gender.

The majority of the sexual messages at work were shared by men and women. Other lesser patterns emerged – of equal opportunities (although mainly related to gender), sexual innuendo, and 'don't mix business with pleasure'. The men offered work messages about male and female chauvinism and to beware of female guile, and homosexuality. Only the category of feeling 'marginalised by men' was noted solely by women.

The managers came from both open and closed organizations, but the findings were not specific to either the organizational settings or any particular profession or work setting.

Shared sexual messages

Gender issues
What are the sex stereotyping and gender issues that affect both men and women managers at work? Gender is certainly an issue for many managers and continues to categorise men and women into certain roles. [44]

> . . . *both girls and boys believe that girls like to play with dolls, help mother, never hit, say 'I need some help' and will grow up to be nurses or teachers, whilst boys like to play with cars, help father, build things, say 'I can hit you' and will grow up to be bosses.*

Parents clearly play a major role in how they influence children's sex roles. Examples of what is said to children, given later in this chapter, emphasise this phenomenon.

The managers' comments supported this notion and they gave examples of how the organizational messages about gender affected them...

> *The sexual messages at work from many male colleagues are that women are to be patronized; that menopausal women are a nuisance; that if you have a professional relationship then you are no fun; and that women take things too seriously at work.*

said Pat and then she went on to distinguish the sexual messages that she picked up from women at work. These were varied for she divided women into two types of behaviour, either offering a supportive relationships or a 'watch your back because you and I are rivals' approach.

This is supported by the comments about different roles; for instance, 'The "girls" teach the soft courses and the men do circuit training and work a lot of unpaid overtime. It is a very macho ethos', stated Kate. But some of the men disagreed, even saying that sex roles did not exist. Bob said:

> *Our messages at work are not at all obtrusive. There is no stereotyping of sex roles, at least none that have provoked comment. However, I do feel personally that sexual attraction does affect and usually facilitates our work relationships, at least in my case it does.*

Some of the men shared the same gender messages. Roy (whose early scripting, was 'men are men') began by saying that he had observed 'No messages from men either towards other men or women' but then went on to say 'No I'm wrong; the messages are "I can cope, let me look after you" from the men.' As far as women were concerned, he commented:

> *The female messages are equally predictable. As a head of the sales department I feel women turn it on to get favours. I've noticed that women give off messages to other women as men do to men.*

Meanwhile, Alan said that his messages were confused. He used the phrase 'Prima Gravida', which is often used to describe women having babies later in life rather than at the expected age. In this case he used the phrase to describe how the organization was late in bringing about new ideas and practices.

> *The 'Prima Gravida' organization is becoming more liberal but old stereotypes still remain. I feel it will take some time for tokenism to be replaced by equality. However, the culture is changing progressively. In my opinion males and females have a tendency to play games.*

The situation was viewed by Tony as 'little girls and boys together and we have to be very careful, even though the equal opportunities organization is weak.'

In terms of gender with reference to equal opportunities Graham was vehement with a disgruntled edge in his voice: 'I don't hear messages other than the overriding message about equality.'

Derek, whose early scripting was that he associated boys with masculinity, virility, power and a macho image, and girls with femininity, weakness and subservience, echoed some of this in his perception of sexual messages at work. He commented 'Respect women or else! Male chauvinism still abounds; beware of feminine guile. Female chauvinism exists.' Arnold's response was 'Done well, flirting can be used by a female to make work more enjoyable.' This man started his life with the early message that nice girls did not have anything to do with sex.

Keith and Peter specifically referred to gender in their responses. These were, from Keith:

> *Women are definitely thought to be suited to inferior roles by many. It is harder for women to be taken seriously as key staff, and some of them actually encourage this. I find sexuality generally helps me get*

on better with women at work, so we can establish a more relaxed and informal relationship – friends as well as colleagues.

and from Peter:

There is a generally friendly banter. It is fairly relaxed and we have close relationships, without sex being involved. I consciously avoid sexual situations at work. I despise a certain female member of staff, but not on sexual grounds. I would feel the same if it was a male in the same position.

The question itself allowed people to talk about what they wanted to talk about, in that some people introduced the element of affairs, intimate touching and sexual relationships. Some of these have links with the following tales about sexuality at work.

Equal opportunities

With the implementation of more policies on all aspects of equal opportunities, gender, race, sexual orientation and the socially and physically disadvantaged, it is not surprising that this category emerged in the study.

'At my present place of work I feel that sexual attitudes are mainly uncomfortable. I feel that despite equal opportunities policies, colleagues are embarrassed and uncomfortable with overt signs of different attitudes to male and female roles,' thought Barbara. 'Equal Opportunities are important,' deliberated Sheena. 'Officially the message is equality, but practically women do not progress as readily,' snapped Janet.

The remainder of the category indicated other aspects of equal opportunities, including positive discrimination, sexual innuendoes, touching statements. Lynn said that the managers were:

generally unbiased. Some men feel they have a right to be closer to me than I think they should – with sexual overtones. Some staff think that women progress due to positive discrimination. Generally I would say that overall my sexuality is a benefit to me although I never (I think) make use of it in that way.

'Women are either decorative or threatening and behaviour in the staff room mainly reflects this,' declared Liz. However, Don decided that:

There are none (sexual messages) when serious matters are being discussed, but when it comes to matters which are more trivial about which there can be a more light-hearted approach, then sexual innuendoes and bantering is commonplace with some men, despite equal opportunities. Since I do not find this offensive, maybe even enjoy the banter, it happens quite frequently. It is harmless and generally makes most people feel good. (I wonder how he knows this?)

Whereas some of the men offered 'It's OK to flirt. I use careful innuendoes but there is an invisible line you should not pass when relating to members of the opposite sex. I think touching is OK within bounds' 'What you do in private is your own affair but don't acknowledge it publicly', quoted Kath. 'Leave sex outside the workplace', [35] stated Margaret, whereas Geoff said 'I am a lone male working in a totally female-dominated section,' so the message is that there are nominal men as well as nominal women and men can be isolated, too. 'I don't think I'm very sensitive about sexual messages. I found them difficult to spot and even more difficult to deal with. I tend to ignore them. I do think that many staff feel that they are useful for the smooth running of the organization,' replied Brian. 'The messages I receive are "Smut" and our male managing director inspires this. The ardent/militant feminists frown on this for their own reasons. I sense that most people would deny that sex exists at all for them,' Mark sneered sarcastically.

Don't mix business with pleasure
This was a category that emerged often in the research for men and women. It is highlighted here by Bernadette, Eileen, Tom and John. Bernadette said she would never be involved with anyone at work as she does not fancy people in the same area of work – banking. 'Men tend to be rather boring in our field but even if I did fancy any of them I wouldn't go out with them because most dates are short-lived relationships and then you have to face them at work when things get nasty. No, not for me ever again. I've learnt my lesson at the last place I worked'.

Eileen thought that the organization's message was 'Don't mix business with pleasure' as she believed this got in the way of trying to be objective in a management post. This is difficult if you are sexually involved with any other staff, senior or junior to you. However, she strongly disagreed with the saying, as she thought that it was very difficult to keep sexuality out of relationships. Whilst she thought sexuality should not be 'used' because it was manipulative, Tom also stated that he thought it was impossible not to use it, even at a subconscious level. 'All women and men use their sexuality at work,' he said emphatically.

This subconscious level was supported by John with his view:

Consciously I never want to get sexually involved with customers or staff because I am happily married and don't want to spoil that, so I never mix business with pleasure. I think that sometimes I must feel subconsciously sexually attracted to customers and other staff because I get physically excited in certain people's presence.

Shared categories

Homosexuality

Some men and women referred to covert and overt messages about homosexuality. Some were anti- whilst some were positive messages. Often they would be added to other messages received. One man, who was given an early message of 'be a heterosexual', but in childlike language 'boys fight and marry girls – girls cry and look after daddies and babies', heard anti-homosexual messages. As he said, 'whilst we are seen as a tolerant firm because of the nature of our product (hair and beauty products) and we use sex to advertise, nonetheless, the message here is that homosexuals are lesser men. We joke about it sometimes in front of gay colleagues but underneath there is a distaste if not a disgust about them, both for the men and the women. Nobody would overtly say that, of course, but this is confidential.'

A woman who was given an early message of sexual stereotyping 'you are pretty and will grow up into a lovely lady and have lots of little children to look after,' heard one part of several sexual messages at work, to 'avoid those aggressive militant lesbians'. She added that 'they are usually ugly and couldn't get a man if they tried. Although there is one downstairs in the hotel reception. I was amazed when I was told because you wouldn't think she was. . . she's quite pretty with long dark hair.'

Tony talked about the sexual messages he received at work as positive and helpful in his work. His own early childhood message was that it was not talked about, a mystery but not bad. 'Within our organization (solicitors) we need to be legally minded but also be understanding and tolerant, but sometimes it is difficult when you get the skivers or the vexatious litigant.' He spoke of one message being 'there but for the grace of God go I,' to which he added 'I suppose that isn't really a sexual message but in a way it is because there are so many more homosexuals now coming out and I cannot get my head around what or why it is happening. Then there are so many more cases of sexual harassment that we now have to deal with. Whilst we have to be objective, people are often subjective when it comes to others' sexual orientation and sexual behaviour, especially if it is different from theirs. So I always find it helpful to recognise that that could be me when defending people of a different orientation.' Tony's concern for other people's different values and beliefs was also expressed in his stories of sexuality at work.

Sexual innuendoes
Both men and women heard messages full of sexual innuendoes about hetero- and homosexuals. These included, from the males 'women rise to the top on their backs'; 'women prefer male bosses'; 'men don't like working for a lesbian boss'; 'to get on here you need to be young, female and attractive'; and from the women 'men are promoted because they have affairs with other men, but nobody ever seems to think that. It is only women who are accused of having come up via a casting couch, but things are changing.' Other messages in this category were 'white middle-class men are discriminated against', the implication being that black females were promoted; 'Women should be at home looking after children'; 'don't send a boy to do a man's job'. One woman had clearly been given a sexual implication by her line manager of her inferiority to a male colleague.

Fear of HIV
With the rise of discussions in the media about HIV positive personnel and the possible implications at work, this category became stronger over the years of research. Both men and women referred to this sexual message at work. Comments were made by

managers in differing work settings, which included 'beware of AIDS. From a male manager of a nightclub: 'think that everybody is HIV positive', from a male manager in a prison: 'always protect yourself from HIV even with minor cuts', from a female director of nursing: 'the sexual message at work for us is each person is valued for themselves' but there is a fear of HIV amongst the medical and support staff and many people become frightened of being contaminated. From the department of a female manager in social work; 'make sure they know about AIDS. There is so much ignorance about the subject and this just leads to prejudice and fear'; from a manager in a College Health Studies Department: 'AIDS awareness is something we have to teach now. Few of us are qualified, but one sexual message around the department is "beware of AIDS". Youngsters today are missing out on spontaneous lovemaking'; and from a Greek director of a holiday travel business who said he used to have sex with many women on holiday, even married women, but now with AIDS, he doesn't any more.' A catering manager said 'One big sex message at work is 'be careful with AIDS.' With food-making you are always careful but now you have to be extra careful if there are accidents in the kitchen.'

Although in these cases I have indicated the areas and type of profession of the managers, this cannot be used as a mindset common to all managers in that particular work setting. Because of the diversity of sexuality and the diversity of early messages and of the kind of messages heard, it would be unwise to pinpoint certain managerial posts as holding or carrying such messages or views. However, it can be seen that sexual messages about the fear of people being HIV positive is more likely to be perceived as prevalent in certain types of jobs and work settings where accidents or sexual liaisons may be everyday occurrences.

Women managers

Feeling marginalised

The only category that emerged in this section as being experienced solely by the women was that of feeling marginalised by men. Women used different words to express their situation [23] however the following response encapsulates what most of the women reported. Brenda disclosed how she felt marginalised as she recounted her perceived sexual messages at work.

> *There is great harassment, working in a male-oriented environment (this is made up of prison officers and male adult prisoners). The conversation and comments are frequently sexually oriented but amongst the education staff it is not so. There is also an all male-oriented management at our link college and there I feel definitely marginalised.*

Similar comments to this were made by many women in different ways. Some of them spoke of poor self-image in all-male meetings and sexual anxiety in interviews with an all-male interviewing panel:

> *I feel an outsider when I go for interviews. It is evident to me that we must make noises about including women in short lists, but they are really on the periphery*

and the problem of working in all-male offices:

> *I get on well with the men really but I often feel on the edge of their relationships as a woman. The message I have is 'keep your distance, women'.*

There is also concern about being a token woman director of sales. The underlying message for many of the women interviewed was:

You've made it via the casting couch and don't expect us men to involve you in our world. Keep out.

Male managers

Male chauvinism still abounds
Sexuality at work, in terms of messages indicated for some of the men but not highlighted under messages by women, was that male chauvinism still abounds. These messages included 'I work in a so-called equal opportunity profession but that is only on the surface because many men believe that women are inferior. It's usually in the pub that the truth comes out. We have to behave at work, but given a few pints blokes talk about their experiences with women that have been fairly useless. A lot of them are good at their job. I work with one who is great. She is intellectually superior to me but we make a good advertising team because I offer her some restrictions and boundaries so she doesn't go all over the place with her ideas. She agrees with me about this.' 'Most men are chauvinistic, is the message I receive' and 'Men make better managers. Women and men prefer to work for men' and 'Men are more reliable and less emotional' were other messages that men heard at work.

Female chauvinism exists
The greater majority of the men in the study were white middle-class males so, in some cases there was a resentment of female line managers, especially if men had been overlooked for promotion, or affirmative action had been taken to establish an equal opportunities policy within an organization. This therefore led to a perception by

some men that promotion was given to women first because of their sex, not because of their ability.

Sexual messages received in this category included 'Woman are promoted here'; 'Women think they are better than the men'; 'Be a Thatcher woman'; 'Women think they are superior to men but you should hear them bitching about each other'; 'Feminists are frightening, is one message at our place. Some of them are more chauvinistic than men ever are or ever have been.'

Beware of female guile
'Watch your back; she takes no prisoners' is the message I get at work about our managing director but she can also be charming and use her feminine guile when she wants you to work overtime or head another one of her immediate new projects' was one man's received message. 'Women can be full of bullshit when it comes to how hard done by they are but I've watched some of them mince their way up to the top, playing little girl lost and daddy's girl. You should see one of the women simpering up to senior men in our organization whom the other men here would be terrified to argue with or take on', was one message. Others were 'A lot of women are full of female guile when it comes to getting on in the firm. The message I get is to beware of women who smile but knife you in the back in front of the managing director,' and 'Women flirt to get what they want.'

Further to these examples is an underlying conflict where the men had recalled early childhood messages that women should know their place and that men should be macho. So many men in this age range were having to be the pioneers in working with women as their line managers yet holding deeply set beliefs that those same women really should be at home doing female tasks. The next generation of men may not have the same conflict, as early messages may have changed.

The sexual messages are overtly or covertly experienced by almost every manager. Even those who began with 'I don't listen to, or don't know' soon added provisos.

Checking messages for their basis in reality is difficult unless all members of an organization were to be interviewed to establish if people were hearing what they wanted to hear, or talking about themselves but using others as a means to say what they believe. We usually say more about ourselves, than we ever do about others, when we talk about other people.

So the categories that emerged from the sexual messages at work are as follows.

Table 4. Analysis of sexual messages at work

WOMEN	SHARED	MEN
Feeling marginalised by men	Gender roles and issues	Male chauvinism still abounds
	Equal opportunities	Female chauvinism exists
	Don't mix business with pleasure	Beware of female guile
	Homosexuality	
	Sexual innuendoes	
	Fear of HIV	

What are the stories of sexuality at work?

As with the other sections, some stories were only told by women or only by men, whilst other stories were shared. Although these stories are written in a different format they are analysed in the same way at the end of the chapter to demonstrate which are shared and which are not.

MANAGER'S PERCEPTIONS ABOUT SEXUALITY AT WORK

A rich variety of tales were told. As Martin [45] suggests, a 'uniqueness paradox' exists since all managers thought that their story was unique but many were duplicated – the names were different but the stories were similar. The stories are broken down into:

1. Confessional Tales [46]
2. Realistic Tales [46]
3. Rule Breaking by High Status People [45]

In their research Harrison & Lee [12] used the stories that subjects told them about other people rather than stories about themselves. Here I use their model of categorising sexual stories and sexual messages about other people, to demonstrate how sexuality affects managers at work. Unlike Harrison & Lee, I use both stories of others and the sexual stories that managers told about themselves.

Confessional tales
Most of these stories fell in to the category of affairs, supporting the work of Quinn & Lees [20]. Both the sexes made reference to the aspect of affairs. Tina commented 'My boss still finds me attractive – we went out together some time ago but; I am a "strong" woman.' 'Equal opportunities are important', said Susie, 'but sometimes you have to make up to men to let them think you might give in until you get your promotion.'

'Women are oppressed by factors such as having very poor maternity leave and lower salaries because of their lower office status, so having affairs is one way of getting "in the know". One of our managers uses her sexuality to oppress her staff who are mainly male', said Clare. 'She had an affair with one of them which caused all kinds of anger amongst the team'.

Rohan said 'We have a friendly unit, where no subject is banned and lots of sexual banter goes on. Affairs happen, people move on.

MANAGER'S PERCEPTIONS ABOUT SEXUALITY AT WORK

In our FE college there is a male establishment in management who appear paternalistic. Nevertheless, my predecessor married a retiring principal...!'

Philip thought that an affair shouldn't happen and then when it does between staff and students it should be kept secret. 'It could ruin your chance of promotion, even though half the staff are married to ex-students.' Interestingly, his early script had been 'Be careful, otherwise you'll have to get married and then pretty women will ruin your career prospects.' This would be borne out with his present perception of what messages are around him. This sounds like he is hearing his 'parental' early messages in an organizational setting.

When Colin started to tell his story, he referred to his early teenage feelings. This seemed to be a way of painting the backcloth for the way he now thought, behaved or felt about his sexuality in his work-place.

> *When I was 16 I was terrified by women. I was married at 21 but this did not change my fear of women. They seemed to haunt the world. I remember one old bat was rumoured to be having it off with a docile male in the filing room.*

The language that he used seemed to underpin his terror of women and that men are the docile partners in sexual relationships. When Colin recalled his sexual messages at work he had said that the message was 'smutty' which was frowned on by the ardent militant feminist for their own reasons. Again his language indicates this same underlying belief that women are terrifying. Happily he went on to talk about how he had changed.

> *All this changed for me when I was training to be a teacher between the ages of 27 and 30. For the first time I began to come to terms with my own feminine side by really talking to fellow female students.*

MANAGER'S PERCEPTIONS ABOUT SEXUALITY AT WORK

Whilst Colin was at college he was also involved in 'a mystical bride and groom ceremony with the art tutor' from whom he still receives poison pen letters, although by now she is over 70 years old.

Colin had more to say on sexuality at work. 'Prior to my arrival at Green Water College it was apparently the case that sex was rampant between staff and staff, and between staff and students. It's all very tight-lipped now. I taught for five years in a college of education where the Head of English picked an annual 'bird' and took her all the way. I myself was ravished in this way and now I've been very happily married for ten years with the woman who pulled me. She is dominant and satisfies all my fetishes.' Colin, in response to his first sexual experience claimed that he preferred women who made the running is borne out in the statement. Again the influence of early childhood sexual experiences appears to affect individuals as adults and is well documented.

Some women admitted to using their sexuality at work for various reasons. Rhona said that she was always aware of males around her. She had had an affair with a co-worker. Jane admitted that she always uses her sexuality, then added rather defiantly 'As a woman I go against all my stated principles of feminism to get my own way'. She went on to add that the more intense relationships became, then, naturally, the people tried harder to hide the affairs but that was because people know each other very well and their secrets were easily discovered.

Ann had had a three-year affair with a married colleague 20 years prior to our meeting. However, since her marriage 17 years ago she had never been tempted to get involved with anyone at work. I thought at this point she was qualifying her statement, as if she had been tempted by someone outside her working environment. Ann went on to emphasise that she had never felt threatened or exploited at work.

Then there were the affairs that women referred to when they were students. 'When I was at university I slept my way through to a 2:1. It was easy. We, the women, all knew which of the men were easy meat. Strange, isn't it, that 'easy' is usually used for women. I wonder what the male equivalent is?' This was Mary's recollection. It is interesting to note here how stereotyping underpins so many of the comments made by the managers. On the other hand, Norma had the opposite experience:

My supervisor made it clear to me that if I had sex with him I'd get a first. I told him to sod off. Isn't it disgraceful that predatory men can get away with such things! Still, that was before such things as sexual harassment were taken seriously. A bit like child abuse – until someone has the guts to say something I suppose it will just go on. I know I didn't tell anyone, probably because if I had got a first then everyone would have assumed it was because I had been to bed with him. I see this happening here (in college) to a lesser extent, although I can't be sure it's not just what the students imply in jest. I don't look into it to see if it's serious. I don't want to get involved.

Yet again, in this story the 'turn a blind eye' syndrome appears.

Realistic tales

Keeping up appearances
It is commonly accepted that there are gender issues in management and managers need to be seen to be non-sexist. Among the reasons for this may be the legal introduction of equal opportunities policies. However, in practice, few things have changed, as is pointed out by Keith. 'I have known a managing director admit that he would short-list women only for the sake of appearances, not as serious candidates. I have known several overtly sexist men co-operate.' Peter

endorsed this with his story of his managing director: 'I perceive within my managing director a need to employ, at all costs, a woman to appear sexually equal in a male-dominant group.' Peter talked about his previous place of employment where two men were hated by female office staff. Their personal workspace was closed down in a threatening manner by these two men, whilst Peter thought that he himself tended to get on well with the women. Possibly they felt safe with him as he was a homosexual.

Managers are having to keep up appearances in terms of the messages they give out. Bridget indicates this: 'In theory my organization is very tolerant and open-minded, but in practice men are powerful. Homosexuality is not acceptable and women use sex to gain access to power.'

Maureen's down-to-earth tale was about sexual harassment. 'When I was younger and first in a working environment, between the age of 16 and 18, I found it difficult to side-step the office groper without confrontation. I've developed this as I've got older and now feel more than capable of dealing with the men — so they now know where they stand — but in such a way that we can still work together. A man I once worked for was accused of sexual harassment and almost lost his job for indulging in sexually orientated banter with a junior female staff member, who wrote down everything he said. Having worked for several years with this man and never at any time felt under threat of a physical nature from him, I felt desperately sorry that this woman would be prepared to ruin a man's career for what amounted to little more than his way of joking. It made me realise not everyone sees things the same way. I still can't make up my mind who was right — him or her?'

Irene's story was that of an all-male senior management team whose working relationships were blocked because of the 'Leg-over Challenge Stakes'. 'None of them are prepared to withdraw from the game.'

'I am perceived as efficient, organised, good at my job. Surprising for a woman, isn't it,' Pat sarcastically added. 'Women in our organization have had to specialise to get into middle management posts.' Kate offers a different view: 'The usual tales of female promotion at our place reflect their sexual partners rather than their ability.'

Lynn's story was 'I know other women in senior posts who feel the same as me. I don't know whether it is me or the system that makes me feel I have to take everything on because I'm a woman. I feel that I have to be careful in the way that I perform so that if I become too angry, or can't take on everything, it may reflect on me as a woman. I can't work out how much this is me and how much is the system. Is it that we needed that drive to break through in years gone by and now have forgotten how to stop?'

Barbara's comment was that 'In a mainly female organization, the two senior posts were held by men. One of these men frequently used a strategy of 'Don't ask me to explain, trust me' to justify his actions and most of the staff did that and were hostile to those women who challenged him.' This was contrary to Don's story: 'Women are still concerned about male power and domination in the workplace. Men sometimes wonder what all the carry on is about. Generally in my own work place I think relations between the sexes are better than good and striving towards a happy partnership.'

One woman's story about another woman was Jan's. 'Open affairs are condemned at our place but it is a lot of pretence really. One female head of department is very powerful and uses her sexuality to create fear among her staff. As a result she is very rude and universally disliked.'

'Some people have got away with a lot, and taken risks, like having relationships between staff taking place during residential management training sessions or conferences in the presence of customers', Kath moralised. This story was duplicated in detail by one of the case studies (Steve), given in Chapter 6.

Philip's stories were part confessional. 'I've tried to find colleagues to go out with but have never succeeded. I've tried not to go out with students but have had three love affairs, one lasting over two years. There was a big scandal at work involving an assistant principal and a student. Also a colleague was given early retirement for allegedly fondling a girl student, though no charges were ever brought. There is also the story of a colleague who sleeps with most of his girl students apparently.'

The reality of sexual attraction was an issue for Bob who was anxious, as he said:

I have been forced recently to accept that I must share a room with a colleague who has indicated that she is in some way attracted to me. The feeling is not reciprocated. I am not looking forward to the reorganization.

and Don who thought:

I worry about giving the wrong messages and being considered sexist. I enjoy the company of women and like working with them. We can learn a great deal from each other.

or:

There are hundreds of stories at work. A curious case is the quite attractive man who spent so much time sexually harassing many of the women. The strange thing was the collusion of the women who seemed to like the attention despite the embarrassment that it must have caused.

Derek's story included the statement 'many women, like men, don't allow their space to be invaded. Affection is often misconstrued as sexual aggression.'

MANAGER'S PERCEPTIONS ABOUT SEXUALITY AT WORK

'I feel thoroughly institutionalised and have ceased to regard sexuality at work as a problem,' grumbled Geoff.

Roy was cross as he said:

Recently I feel I have been manipulated by a woman who wanted a certain work schedule. I didn't think that she suited this work. She cried and walked out. I felt guilty at first, then bemused, as I thought back to aspects of our previous working relationship which I now suspect was contrived.

From Keith:

I have noticed that those women who have made career progress often, not always, have a masculine air to them. I even know one who makes sexist remarks against females to keep in with her male colleagues!

However, some managers did not have any stories on sexual messages at work. Brian was one of these. 'Although I met my present partner at work, not in my present employment, and I am sometimes attracted to people, I do not have a story. I tend to ignore the signals'.

Some of the managers recounted tales about homosexual men or women, for example, how men had been promoted because they were sexually involved with a male managing director. Also other stories centred on homosexual males being sexually harassed by other male staff to the point where they asked for early retirement or left the company. Lesbians were criticised by women as being 'butch and man-like otherwise they would not have made it in a man's world'. However, there were also some stories about homosexuality being a positive attribute (see Paul in Chapter 6). Other stories were told about how rules are broken and particularly about those people in high ranking positions.

MANAGER'S PERCEPTIONS ABOUT SEXUALITY AT WORK

Rule breaking by high status person
Debbie told the story of her husband (a high status person) who was a professor in child care at a university. He had been sexually interfering with their daughter since she was six years old. Debbie had two daughters and when we first met expressed concern about the younger one. Eventually she found out about the incest from the child's aunt. The husband denies the accusation and says the child is suffering from 'false memory recall syndrome'. He sends academic articles to the mother to say he is innocent. The daughter is still in therapy and the therapist says that she has been destroyed by the father's abuse. Debbie has divorced her husband but part of the divorce settlement package was that she must never tell anyone about her discovery, as he would lose his academic standing. Debbie was off work for several months with stress, but has now returned to full-time work and she also works four evenings a week to pay for her daughter's therapy.

Ann offered four main stories that were being circulated around the organization, one being about their anti-racist managing director's unwelcome intimacy with his black secretaries. A second story was about other staff not accepting that Ann was to go on holiday with a lesbian colleague of a lower work status – earlier the staff had thought she was also breaking social heterosexual rules. Her third story concerned the general disapproval of unmarried colleagues having babies, in particular a senior woman manager, and the fourth was about a male colleague who had left his wife in order to live with another male colleague.

Two stories of upward and downward power were given in relation to deputy managing directors. The upward power story was male: 'One director at one of our offices promoted a science technician to a senior position overnight, then she fell out with him and ran the section as she wanted,' said Ted, who referred to his line manager who 'threatened the director (male) and indirectly the governors that if she was not appointed as deputy in restructuring, she would make an equal opportunities claim and produced the relevant papers.'

Through the bedroom ceiling!
There is a phrase (through the glass ceiling) which refers to the perceived work situation for women, in that they can go so far up the promotion ladder but then reach a glass ceiling which separates them from the senior male managers and is very difficult to break through. In contradiction of this notion it would appear from a number of the stories that some women are supposedly promoted from the bedroom. These stories were told by women and men. Saskia volunteered, 'There are the usual tales of female promotion being because of their sexual partners rather than their ability.' Delia offered, 'We had a part-time member of staff who rapidly became full-time and with a position of responsibility. Then she became the fifth wife of the sales director.' Rule breaking by a high status person appears in these stories to be mainly having a man as the high status person, although with more female senior managers being appointed this may apply to women in the next few decades and is already happening in America.

Finally as the head of personnel of one large distribution firm said 'Sexual stories abound here; everyone talks about sex but our policy is we know it's going on but if you don't ask any questions then you don't have to do anything about it.'

So what are the shared stories and experiences of the managers? Here I highlight the differences and similarities of sexual stories and sexual messages as perceived by the individuals.

Table 5. Sexual stories of managers – shared and separate experiences

WOMEN	SHARED EXPERIENCES	MEN
Achieving acceptable and unacceptable female promotion	Keeping up appearances	Confessional tales of affairs with customers
Using their sexuality at work	Gender issues	Experienced being anxious about how to behave towards women
Being propositioned by men	Sexual harassment	Wished to exhibit the feminine side of themselves
	Affairs between managers and colleagues	
	Rule breaking by high status people	
	Through the bedroom ceiling: promotion through affairs	

What aspects of working life are identified where sexuality does affect the managers?

This study now unveils some of the areas and situations at work where managers do think that their sexuality affects them.

I begin by giving examples of specific areas and categories that are identified where sexuality affects aspects of their work, both genders women or men only. These include promotions, meetings, feeling uncomfortable, interviews and the presence of sex typing and projection. Then I illustrate how some managers said whether they were frequently affected, or not, by their sexuality in the work setting.

Both genders

Promotions

A number of managers (13%) admitted to being 'sexually' involved with staff who held influential positions, with the result that this proved an advantage or disadvantage at some point in their careers.

Neil Lyndon [47] recognises the existence of sexual involvement of line managers and how that may affect work but he also thinks that as a man this also works with males in terms of friendship.

> *A sexual relationship might develop between myself and the woman I was working with. That explosive element of chance has made some difference to my fortunes but not much, I feel. Perhaps I have been given work by a few women who wanted to advance a personal connection. I may have been refused some work by women who did not relish the closer connection I fancied. Perhaps I have been denied work by women who were offended by my unwillingness to get into bed with them or by some who were not pleased by my behaviour when we got there or afterwards.*

Lyndon admits that his sexual involvement with some of his female line managers brought both rewards and retribution depending on the success or otherwise of his liaison. This sentiment was echoed by one male manager, saying:

> *My sexuality most certainly affects me at work, because of my affair with Norma. She was instrumental in my promotion, although she would deny it. I look forward to Mondays when I will see her. She makes me feel alive and worthwhile!*

One woman added to this idea of reward or retribution in her particular perception:

Sometimes it all seems great and I think this really is what life is all about, being wanted and sexually attractive to him and other men, but at other times I feel like a whore, using my body to get what I want, a promotion, status or a more taxing area of work. Sometimes I feel guilty, especially when he shows favouritism towards me in meetings but that's when he's feeling positive about me. But again there are occasions when he deliberately puts me down in front of other staff if our sexual relationship is rocky. Then I feel angry. I suppose I have no right to, but I do.

In meetings

Sexuality probably affects a lot of managers in meetings even when they have not been sexually involved with someone present in the group. The ways in which managers were affected by their sexuality in meetings is highlighted by the comments from both women and men where they indicated there were a wide range of emotions: feelings of being dismissed because of their gender, being marginalised, feeling second class, needing support and/or being sexually aroused.

Half of the women interviewed referred to their sexuality affecting them in meetings.

I feel definitely second class in management meetings where I am the only woman. I argue for 'people' and 'caring' and my views are dismissed. Also in my appraisal I identified counselling as an important aspect of my work but the firm won't find the funds to support it.

In meetings where there are conflicts of opinion with a male I am conscious that I need support from other women to stand firm. It is usually in public meetings that this is a problem. I feel as though I can cope in a one-to-one situation.

Only a third of the men admitted that their sexuality affected them in meetings. One man mentioned his sexual excitement in meetings:

> *I feel I can discuss more intimately with female colleagues. I relate more to women with maternal feelings (but not male managers with paternal feelings). I am excited in some meetings with women but have not made decisions in favour of women or pointedly against. Well, I don't think I have.*

It is worth noting that, as in this example, the majority of men would justify their comments about their sexuality.

Some managers felt uncomfortable about their sexuality
This may be because of the sex role messages of their early childhood, as demonstrated by the comments that both women and men shared about their sexuality. 'As a woman I feel inferior. I'm wary of projecting the incorrect image and stance.' Maybe this woman was trying to please others or maybe again attempting to play out her 'correct' female image and stance given to her in early messages.

> *Being male, and all of my bosses being male, usually sexuality is not a factor, although I must admit that I wish I felt able to be more emotional at times with them. I find women generally very much easier to work with. I come from an all-female family with no father or uncles but lots of aunts and this is probably the reason. I find it difficult talking with men or women if they are upset. One woman was crying once about the death of her father and I was able to hold her gently and comfort her. But on another occasion I was talking to one of my male staff, who was upset and cried but I was useless. I felt embarrassed for him.*

This example illustrates how the childhood message of 'little boys don't cry' may later affect the manager.

Both sex stereotyping and sexual attitudes are apparent in one statement: 'My sexuality depends on the individual but I feel very uncomfortable if a female becomes aggressive.' I believe that most men do show their feelings, but they show them in different ways from women. This theme is developed in the next section of the chapter. What is evident from these findings is the reference that many managers make to the way in which their sexuality has been influenced by attitudes acquired in childhood.

Sexual stereotyping came from both genders as can be seen throughout the book but also there was one category of sex typing and projection that emerged just in men's comments. It can also be seen in the interview category relating to women managers.

Women managers

Interviews
Two-fifths of the women managers referred to interviews as a forum for the effects of their sexuality. Some women commented on the advantages of being a woman at an interview and admitted to using their 'sexuality'; others referred to how they dressed; whilst others tried to work out if it was them or the system that made them take on everything. 'I'm not sure if my sexuality affects me, although as a woman I was surprised that in interviews I was told I was too aggressive,' was a comment from a female, surprised since it is usually to men that words like aggressive are attributed. Furthermore:

> *In interviews I use my attractiveness as an extra tool for success. Why the hell not! I feel if I become more successful or responsible I may have to change my appearance to gain respect or be seen as powerful. But I don't want to start power dressing and have my hair cut short. I need to learn skills for this rather than rely on appearance, to use my sexuality positively.*

Being a woman appeared to bring special difficulties for some of the managers. 'In interviews I think that I am not being taken seriously as a woman; my contributions are not valued.' 'I am seen as feminist and therefore suspect in interviews' and 'In interviews, I feel I am more prepared to give other women with children or of child-bearing age more consideration.' Again sex typing was prevalent and bears out sex roles that are attributed to men and women which may be particularly frequent in interviews.

However, a few of the women did refute the idea that their sexuality affected them in interviews.

> *Other than the fact that all staff are dealt with in the same way, I do not feel that sexuality affects me in interviews whether they are male or female. I tend to deal with people as individuals.*

Male managers

Sex typing and sexual projection
Some of the men added to the theory of sex typing and projection by saying how their sexuality did not affect them but did affect others. They said how in people management it was often difficult to interact on the basis of equality because males and females both brought sexual prejudices into the situation. Also 'I am not aware of sexuality affecting me, nor has it been brought to my attention other than I am afraid of being at the receiving end of an accusation or prejudice', but 'It may affect my colleagues more than I feel it affects me.' One man said that he thought that he had progressed in his career 'better than I would have been allowed to as a woman', while another commented on gender influences: 'I am at ease with my sexuality and it does not affect me at work. Sometimes my gender influences certain situations both positively and negatively outside

work. My preference is to be relatively natural and I find people who are ill at ease with their sexuality to be problematic.'

Many managers share the experience of being affected by their sexuality

Although this research is of a qualitative nature certain figures have been obtained. In quantitative terms (to the nearest percentage) 91% of all the managers stated that they were affected by their sexuality. Of those, 44% thought that they were frequently affected, whilst 9% thought that their sexuality did not affect them at work at all. Certainly there was an acceptance that this phenomenon *did* exist. Both men (85) and women (93) admitted to being frequently affected. The women managers who thought that they were greatly affected by their sexuality at work highlighted different ways in which they felt that this happened.

> *I'm sure that sexuality affects me greatly. If I find a person attractive in the broadest sense then I like them and work well with them and vice versa. Being aware of this I try to equalise my behaviour. I do tend to like most people.*

As sexuality has such a wide meaning, semantics were important for some people.

> *I use my femininity, not sexuality in my interactions. I do manipulate men by my manner but it's not little girlish. I'm not sure what it is, I just feel I manipulate them in a different way to women. That's why I prefer to work with men; I feel more comfortable and powerful.*

This last comment adds to the notion that sex is powerful [60]). The notion that sexuality can also have a positive effect at work [61] is shown by comments like 'I play each situation by ear. I do use my sexuality to help me oil the wheels to some extent. I think that is OK,' and 'I feel that men between 35 and 65 like me quite a lot. I suspect this has made things easier for me with interviews and exams.'

A further comment that highlights other women's stories was:

> *There was no way I would have been promoted unless I had had sex with the managing director. I really dislike him but I was ambitious. You might as well do it because that's what other staff think is going on anyway.*

Meanwhile, male managers agreed that they were frequently affected by their sexuality at work and related other incidents but tended to justify their comments – unlike most of the women, who openly admitted their sexual behaviour without excuses. 'Naturally there are girl students I want. But it is because I know I want them that I impose a scrupulously fair assessment process and remain objective. Do you think that this is possible?' (As he asked me to confirm his statement I heard his own disbelief in his behaviour.)

The element of attractiveness was a shared perception by some of the men.

> *I am undoubtedly attracted to and favour those of the opposite sex who are good looking, all else being equal. However, I believe that it does not dominate my judgement. As in social contacts, I enjoy relations more with colleagues whom I value or admire or those to whom I am attracted.*

There are mixed messages in this response, a desire by the man to give off a 'macho' image of himself but with a suggestion that he needed to use his 'feminine' side so he was attractive to both sexes.

I expect that I give off the right signals to show that I am confident, have ability, and very competent. Also I believe in a non-aggressive way and I am anti the traditional male hierarchy stuff. I do this to be attractive both to women and to men with whom I wish to work. I think I am an attractive personality, so this must involve sexuality.

He was certainly aware of himself and struggled with his own sexuality, permitting his 'feminine' side to emerge, but simultaneously wanting to be one of the men. This justification of sexuality continues with a further response: 'I think that all women have qualities of their own.'

A further justification can be seen with the following:

I feel I may be swayed by a flashing smile or a good pair of legs but I try to be objective and look at qualities by which I can evaluate all staff whether they are male, female or homosexual.

(This seems a strange way to categorise people but then this person had received early messages that homosexuality was 'wrong'.) Sexual stereotyping was evident in the following denial and admissions of the affects of sexuality at work. 'Sexuality does not affect me as such except in the general need to represent a strong male stoical image: that is, I try not to get upset over anything.'

'Sometimes I find it hard to tell female staff that their work is poor, especially if they are very pretty.' Another response was:

I recognise it as an integral part of my relationship with all colleagues. I am attracted by people, I try to figure out why I am repelled by some and take steps to attract and be attracted. I enjoy relating both to women and men. My working partner and I frequently give each other hugs over successes and miseries. I chose to appoint her because I was attracted by her aura but I have no desire for sex with her. Her Roman Catholic principles cause her to wax very prudish and I'm quite surprised she's so huggish. She thought that my writing to you about my sexual stories was filthy!

This supports early comments and childhood messages on how the Church may influence sexual attitudes.

The way in which 89 men revealed how they were greatly affected by their sexuality at work is captured by 'I am certainly affected by my sexuality. There have been many women at work whom I have had sexual liaisons with in the past but now we are good friends. We've seen too many of our colleagues have breakdowns. Once I appointed a woman because she reminded me of my first lover. We had sex in the first few months she was here.'

In distinct contradiction to these comments there were only a few managers [36] who were not sure if their sexuality did affect them at work and these included comments made by two women. 'I think I can honestly say not at all.' And 'It doesn't affect me at all to my knowledge.' Whilst the comments made by men were 'Not that I know of' and 'I am not aware of any ways in which my sexuality affects me at work. Perhaps I ought to change sex and see if it makes any difference to me or others.'

So how does sexuality affect managers at work?

Table 6. How sexuality affects managers at work

WOMEN ONLY	BOTH GENDERS	MEN ONLY
In addition to the possibility of gaining promotion,. Many (two-fifths) of the women admitted that they were affected by their sexuality in INTERVIEWS and in terms of how they DRESS both in interviews and at work	As well as the way in which the list of sexual messages and sexual stories at work are affecting managers, both genders admitted their sexuality affected them: in PROMOTIONS in MEETINGS in FEELING UNCOMFORTABLE about their sexuality and by STEREOTYPING The great majority of managers (91%) were affected by their sexuality, while a minority (9%) thought that their sexuality did not affect them at all at work	Further to affairs with customers, anxious about relating to women and chauvinistic thinking, three-quarters of the male managers JUSTIFIED their sexual behaviour when talking about their sexuality at work and over half PROJECTED their sexuality onto others

Summary

The results of the survey have been collated and are presented on the next two pages in a comprehensive table (Table 7).

Table 7a. Analysis of sexual messages

WOMEN ONLY	BOTH GENDERS	MEN ONLY
Sex is for marriage, so one should wait Sex has to be endured Sex is embarrassing - be modest	Sex is not talked about Sex is wicked Sex has religious warnings Women are supreme temptresses Sex is enjoyable – BUT Sex can ruin your career Don't do it Nice girls don't Boys do this — girls do that Sex typing and sex roles	Big boys don't cry Be a macho man Be heterosexual, don't deviate Homophobic messages

Table 7b. Attitude changes

WOMEN ONLY	BOTH GENDERS	MEN ONLY
More women (80%) experienced a change in attitude	Attitude changes	Fewer men (20%) experienced a change in attitude
Fewer women (20%) experienced inner conflict	Experienced inner conflict (early sexual messages conflicting with present expected attitudes)	More men (80%) experienced conflict

Table 7c. Summary of first sexual experiences

WOMEN ONLY	BOTH GENDERS	MEN ONLY
Women perceived this to be: Petting Marriage Orgasm Rape	Assault/abuse Full penetrative sex (vaginal/anal) Making links with childhood messages Ageism (larger number of men)	Men perceived this to be: Self and mutual masturbation Discovering their own sexuality and that of others

Table 7d. Perceived sexual messages at work

WOMEN ONLY	BOTH GENDERS	MEN ONLY
Feeling marginalised by men	Gender roles and issues Equal opportunities Don't mix business with pleasure Homosexuality Sexual innuendoes Fear of HIV	Male chauvinism still abounds Female chauvinism exists

Table 7e. Sexual stories at work were about. . .

WOMEN ONLY	BOTH GENDERS	MEN ONLY
Achieving a genuine promotion by unfair means	Keeping up appearances	Recorded confessional tales of affairs with customers
Using their sexuality at work	Gender issues	Experienced being anxious about how to behave towards women
Being propositioned by men	Affairs between managers and colleagues	Wished to exhibit the feminine side of themselves
	Rule breaking by high status people	
	Through the bedroom: promotion through affairs	

Table 7f. How sexuality affects managers at work

WOMEN ONLY	BOTH GENDERS	MEN ONLY
In addition to the possibility of gaining promotion, many (two-fifths) of women admitted that they were affected by their sexuality in INTERVIEWS and in terms of how they DRESS both in interviews and at work	As well as the way in which the list of sexual messages and sexual stories at work are affecting managers, both genders admitted their sexuality affected them: in PROMOTIONS in MEETINGS in FEELING UNCOMFORT-ABLE about their sexuality and by STEREOTYPING The great majority of managers (91%) were affected by their sexuality, whilst a minority (9%) thought that their sexuality did not affect them at all at work	Further to affairs with customers, anxious about relating to women and chauvinistic thinking, threequarters of the male managers JUSTIFIED their sexual behaviour when talking about their sexuality at work and PROJECTED their sexuality on to others

CHAPTER 6

CASE STUDIES

The following ten case studies were chosen because they represent different themes and different types of experiences of sexuality at work. Eight of the stories are written in question and answer form and two are written in story form. I have transcribed the interviews, using the exact words and phrases that were used by the people chosen. Some of the language may be unfamiliar to the reader as some local idioms were used and the responses were not always in full sentences.

Although only ten people were selected, they represented different types of managers, work roles, sexual orientation, organizations, vocational backgrounds, ages, races, genders, attitudes, educational and social backgrounds, marital status and personality types. These ten people are significant and recurring within the sample of managers interviewed. I do not wish to be more specific for fear of identifying too clearly the individuals selected.

The accounts are written chronologically and thematically. They look at past sexual experiences, present work situations and also to the future, where possible changes may occur. These may be the result of connections which individuals have made with their past sexual scripts and where they have chosen to change them, or a conscious appraisal of how their sexuality at work is affecting their lives (either negatively or positively).

CASE STUDIES

The selected managers – six men and four women – were also from the North West, North East, the West Midlands, South West and South Eastern parts of the UK. The summary at the end of this chapter gives the specific reasons for choosing these particular case studies.

★ ★

1. Nick – naughty but nice

Nick was tall, childlike, full of mischief and describes himself as a free spirit. He is caring, compassionate and sensitive about most of the people to whom he refers in his stories.

I explained as I did with all the interviews that I would be asking questions about his past recalled sexual messages and experiences, stories about himself and others at work, sexual messages at work and if his sexuality affected him at work.

I reassured him of the confidentiality of the interview and that I would send him a copy for him to change should he want to. I said I would change his name and others in the stories again to preserve confidentiality. With this he said 'You can call me Nick. No one would know me by that. When I was young I called myself Oliver, Richard, Graham, Andrew, Sebastian, Mark and put it on forms so when my initials came out I had ORGASM.'

Early sexual experiences

His early recalled messages were:

> *'Nothing from my mum and dad. There was a lack of anything said to me about sex or sexuality. My mum was 40 when she had me. I was the last of seven and the only knowledge I had was that sex produced children. All the messages were negative about sex from Church and from the teachers at my Roman Catholic school. I felt a sense of fudging as if there was a crossing of wires. The reason being*

that I was receiving different pieces of knowledge from friends. It was naughty but nice. There was conflict there. What the people in authority were saying to me I believed them, but I was also hearing 'do it anyway!' which I did. Oh, the guilt afterwards.

I asked Nick about his first sexual experience. He answered quickly, with a delighted expression as he recalled it.

It was with a girl; we were exploring. I was between five and eight. I don't connect that with feeling bad; there was no guilt. I know that was my age on the basis of where I lived. I remember her name. There was no guilt because it may have been before I was being told it was bad. People probably thought I was too young to be given sex messages then. Remember the idea then was 'Don't talk to kids too young otherwise they'll want to do it.' I remember such guilt about masturbation. I thought I was going to Hell. I remember once thinking, the next person I meet, I'm going to throw into a ditch and rape!

Later he told me that, in fact, nobody came along. He went on to say:

You know what Roman Catholics think – the thought is as bad as the act, so I've done it. How could I admit to rape? Having Communion in a state of mortal sin is a worse mortal sin. I was going to different churches thinking, 'Can I go in here and confess?' Eventually I did and the priest said I had 'impure thoughts', whilst I thought I'd done it and committed a mortal sin. Something was saying to me DO IT. I was so obsessed with it especially between 12 and 17.

'What is your attitude towards sexuality now?' I asked.
'I've just realised what my early messages were: good girls don't.

I expect women to hold the same attitude now... that women don't. I don't like to think that but deep in me I think that my wife is doing it to please me not because she really wants to.

'What is your sexual orientation?' I enquired.
'Heterosexual', he replied quickly.

Other men have attempted to force themselves on me. There was one man called Cocky Watchman. He had a caravan. He had a TV in it and we didn't have one then. Once I was on my own with him and he put his hand on my knee. He had warts on his hand and the warts made me feel 'ooh'. Then there was the caretaker, he asked me to help him with the tables at school and he pressed himself against me.

At school there was a high level of homosexual behaviour between the Brothers. One Brother, Gabriel, used to look at your legs and then hit them, then he'd make you sit on his knee on some strange pretext. I was scared of him. He had the power to cane you for your behaviour. Now I realise he was a masochist and what he was doing it for. Then there was also Brother Victor. He used to cane the boys for sexual pleasure. I guess we all knew that but we never said.

'What about your sexuality at work?' I was bringing past memories into the present.

Present sexual experiences

When I worked in the food industry, I slept with someone else. It meant nothing to me other than sex. I was on a course. I told my wife I got drunk and went to bed and had sex. Sophia my wife was pregnant for the second time and I didn't like her being pregnant. She is sexually unattractive when she is pregnant.

CASE STUDIES

'What was your motive for telling her?'

He looked perplexed and anxious. 'My motive for telling her,' he paused and continued:

> *'I couldn't not tell her. There was no way I could live with her and not tell her. I suppose that says more about me than her. Now I know I told her because I was selfish and it made me feel better. Since then when I have been attracted to women at other times I have built up my defences. I felt in control after what happened because at the time I thought I was not in control although I know for me that sex equates with love and I can't have one without the other. I thought that I felt love for her and love allowed me to have sex because I felt love for this person.'*

He looked at me wide-eyed as if to say, 'Do you believe me?' I nodded. He continued. 'I'm scared of touching someone now. I don't want to feel the guilt again.'

'What are the sexual messages in the organization?' I continued. This varied:

> *. . .from those who let their sexual messages out, but do not do anything in the organization, to people within the organization who do have sexual relationships and let it out and others who do but don't talk about it. There is a gossip level. . . those who are having sex and those who want to talk about it and some who are doing it but don't want to talk about it. The word EVIL comes to mind. Some want to talk about it in an evil way.*

'What sexual stories are being told in the organization?' I enquired.

'There are so many,' he began.

> *I suppose they are just the normal stories of people doing something about it (their sexuality), tearing families apart, finding someone else, then breaking up and finding someone else again. Many people just seem to replicate the same experiences, moving from one disastrous relationship to another one. There is a higher level of sexuality about than I expected when I came to this new job in industry. Men like men who hold themselves together and keep away from involvement for fear of the results. I suppose men like having control.*

'Has your sexuality ever affected you at work?' Nick lowered his head, but still looked straight at me. His eyes were still as he recounted his story.

> *There was somebody at work – everything about her was attractive. I was on her interview panel and it would have meant her working with me. It was my influence that stopped her getting the job. It would have been too risky for me because she was so attractive and I had such strong sexual feelings towards her and it would have meant a complete sexual relationship. I've never spoken to her, or anybody else about it until just now with you.*

'Does your sexuality affect you at work?' I watched as he moved his body, enfolding himself with his arms as if to comfort himself.

> *I find it easier to touch men than women. I relate to men in a physical way, because there is no physical attraction. I am very comfortable with all my male colleagues. I am not homosexual. I'm aware of touching a woman member of staff and I ask myself why am I doing it. I cut off from women.*

CASE STUDIES

Future connections

'Having talked with me about your sexuality, have you made any connections with what was and what is now?' I questioned him quietly, having noticed his reactions already as he made the connections between early childhood experiences and his present working life.

Yes, there are a number of connections. Things I have never explored. I've just realised I only touch people that I don't want sexually. I need to realise that when I am working with staff and customers. I now realise that this was what was happening to me when Sophia was pregnant, and how I felt about her sexually and so the reason why I told Sophia about my affair. Articulating the touching bit with you has made me aware of it but I feel that I am at a starting point of trying to deal with it.

'Having made the connections, are there any ways in which you may do anything differently in the future as a result of our interview?' I asked gently.
Nick replied quietly:

I see that it is a ridiculous way of working. I'm in fear of my sexuality: fear of having a normal tactile relationship. I can see now that I know the difference. I'll think about it a bit more. In future I will know there are parts of me that are mature but sexually I feel about six years old and there are parts of me that have not grown up at all.

The interview was drawing to a close when Nick leaned forward enthusiastically and excitedly said 'Can I tell you another story, Jean?'
'Yes, of course,' I smiled.

CASE STUDIES

> *This blew my mind. There were these priests. Father McNulty, he was a real 'all right' person, like an uncle. He stayed with us at home when he was on holiday. One of my sisters was joking about Father McNulty only three months ago. Apparently he went into the girls' bedroom and slept with them. They were aware of what was happening to each other but never told anyone. They used to experience such revulsion after this person came to the house. My sister talked about how fearful she was when she saw the turning of the knob on the door. I can't believe that he did that but I know it's true because all my sisters experienced it.*

He then continued, having relaxed his shoulders.

> *Also there is another one (story). This is about a fat American brother who walked us up the hill. We (Nick's brothers and his sisters) had individual days out with him and he would say 'It's your day' and then we could choose what we wanted on our day. I always chose Vimto. He was fine with me. But when he took my sisters up the hill he used to sexually interfere with them. I find it staggering that that could go on. You know, I've also started thinking about incest. Between one of my sisters and myself. I've always been sexually attracted to her but never done anything about it. But even now, I often think if I could live with anybody I could live with her. We've said that to each other but I've never said the sexual bit to her.*

Nick became very excited as he leaned forward the whole time whilst telling me the last three stories; they just poured out one after the other. When we had finished he took a deep breath and fell back into his chair, smiling and saying 'Thanks for listening'. As we walked out of the private room together he said 'How did I do, am I all right then?'
'Yes of course you are, thank you for such a wonderful, honest, open interview full of rich stories.'

CASE STUDIES

Analysis
Nick embodied Burrell's findings – an early indoctrination of the Roman Catholic Church had left him with the attitude that sexuality 'was bad, even evil, not allowed and was problematical'. He experienced cognitive dissonance after he was told that it was bad. This was when he was masturbating and enjoying the feeling but thinking that he was going to hell. He also experienced cognitive dissonance when he had to deal with two conflicting concepts – that a priest was a good person and that a priest sexually interfered with his sister. He is scared of touching people because he does not want to feel the sense of guilt again and so his male role was not to touch staff or customers. Making connections for Nick is important so he is more likely to change his behaviour. Months later I heard that he was now experiencing a better working relationship especially with the women with whom he works.

★ ★

2. Vivienne – vivacious but virtuous
Vivienne was a tall sylph-like woman with long red hair that bounced whilst she talked. In the interview her face was very expressive and lit up when she was aroused but then would become serious and intent as she intelligently expressed the sadder sexual recollections and thoughts about her future management role. Her tales of the organization management were told in a vivacious, fun loving way but had undertones of criticism, although as she said, 'I like them all', referring to the people in her stories.

Early experiences
'What were your early recalled sexual memories, Vivienne?'
　'None really,' she replied.

CASE STUDIES

I went to a secondary school and that was when I first heard about sex. It was a forward-thinking school and we had this film Susan had a Baby *along with films on VD and sexually transmitted diseases. Mum and Dad thought that it was a good idea. Really it was an asexual message. You know I still feel embarrassed when I watch sex on TV with my mother.*

She stopped speaking and thought for a few moments.

No, my real message was that it was wrong; it should be done privately between two people — not to be talked about, not on TV, radio, books or films. I remember I had no idea where babies came from until secondary school. There was no overt affection between adults around me. I was the eldest of two, with a younger brother. There was lots of affection between parents and children but not between parent and parent.

'What was your first sexual experience?' I continued. Vivienne replied quickly:

With a girlfriend at 14. We pretended each other was a boy, vaguely touched each other for four nights, once on the rib but she thought it was my breast, and then on the breast but nowhere else. Then at 17, with a boy from public school, I was at secondary school and I fancied boys from public school. We lay in a field. It was night time and cold. He undid my coat and blouse and when I stopped him, he expected me to walk home on my own down a dark country lane. I was furious.

'What is your sexual orientation? I enquired, having heard of two experiences involving both genders. 'Heterosexual, apart from the time with my friend Gill, but I believe everyone's got a bit of both,' she spoke quickly throughout the discussion.

CASE STUDIES

Present sexual experiences
'What about now? What do you feel or think about sexuality?'

'It should be discussed; it should be open, with no hang-ups. It should be enjoyed and funny; it can be fun.' This was opposite to earlier scripting of a topic not to be talked about. 'I hope I've not swung away from my parents' views on purpose,' she added, looking straight at me for an answer. I made no immediate comment. She contemplated the possibility, then shook her head and went on wondering if it would have helped her to have explored this avenue of thought.

'Does your sexuality affect you at work?'

'Definitely', she came back quickly and smiling. (This unfortunately was a closed question which had elicited a one-word answer so I continued to explore.) 'How?' I probed.

'I use it, my sexuality I mean, and a lot of the men I know use theirs.'

'In what way?' I urged, seeking specific examples.

I do it openly; they (men) know I'm openly flirting. I use the animal approach. I'm a female and you're a male. Recently when I broke down with the Principal and I was in tears, I was furious because I had gone to see him on an equal level. I thought I was using a female ploy – crying. I want to be in control; I want to be taken seriously.

She continued without further questions to establish the reason for her present construction of sexuality.

I had a bad patch between 13 and 33. I was not too attractive. My husband was the first man to say I'm attractive. It came as a shock, that I was more attractive than I thought and that people do find me attractive, both males and females. I don't think being attractive should be important BUT IT IS.

She emphasised her view with a pointed finger upwards towards the ceiling, a gesture which I had never seen her make before. 'That is true upwards in our Senior Managers Team!'

Present sexuality

'In what ways does your sexuality affect you at work?'

'I'm easier with women than men. Since I found out that I was attractive, my relationships with men have got easier. I use my sexuality.' She referred to the theory of the Johari window (ways of giving feedback to develop unused potential), saying 'You know my public area – they know I know that they know!' (As against the private area where she knows that she is using her sexuality but they [men] don't, or the blind areas where they [men] perceive that she is using it but she isn't.) 'When I interview people I hope I don't use it at all as I now feel equal with men', she admitted, then went on to talk about how her sexuality affected her when she was the person being interviewed. 'When I go for interviews I use it if I think it's going to help.'

'How?'

> *I don't flash a leg; I use it in answer to questions. When I was a senior lecturer I was interviewed for a new post, where I was going to be another woman on the team. The Principal said, 'If I appoint you we'll have an all-female senior management team in that faculty and people will comment.' I said 'If I'm going to be criticised for something it might as well be for something I'm used to being criticised for.' I needed to clarify what she meant and she said 'I mean being criticised for being a woman.' I'm used to that.*

She continued:

> *I used it (sexuality) as an enticement, like a wink. When I was on the directorate, I was the only female and I was also seen as the clown.*

CASE STUDIES

As a woman I could make jokes that others wouldn't make, but I got away with it. I remember at one interview at the place where I was working, I sat there and looked at the senior management team and thought: I don't think you work as a team; you don't look like a team; the only thing you have in common is that you've all got a tie on – and they looked bloody awful. I told them so afterwards and bought them all a decent tie. No one could have done this unless they were a woman. I use humour too, in a sexual manner.

I went on to examine her sexual messages at work. Laughing quickly she responded. 'Not with students! If you do, guess what will happen to you! OK with other members of staff, other staff enjoy that and like the gossip and I do to be honest – I'm probably spreading it. She grinned mischievously. Then with a serious tone to her voice and with a genuine concerned look on her face, as if taking an oath, she said 'I'm the best secret keeper of all if I'm told to keep it quiet!' There was a pause as she reflected. 'But I've got a big mouth if I'm not told to keep it quiet.'

We moved on to the area of story telling. 'What stories of your own sexuality at work would you like to tell me about?'

Vivienne went on to unfold her confessional tale.

Well, as I said, I was at a secondary school for five years and knew nothing. Then I went to college and again I didn't really know anything. At my first school where I worked as a teacher something did happen. Because of my husband's work we had had to move away from an area we loved and temporarily I had to travel two and a half hours to work. I was very depressed and ended up having an affair with the drama teacher – no one knew. Years later (a female), my Head of Department, commented that she thought he'd fancied me but (she) clearly thought nothing had happened. So I was right that no one suspected me.

'Having recalled that time, what are you feeling now?' I gently probed.

I've never regretted it. It is the only affair that I've ever had and it was exciting, it gave me an ego trip — he and his wife only made love about twice a year. He fell in love with me — I didn't with him.

Then I asked Vivienne, 'What about the sexual stories at work about other people?'

She started her story which was full of intrigue, humour, criticism, shock, analysis and compassion.

Mary fancied the Vice Principal, Paul. They got friendly; he asked her home to spend Easter with him and his family. Mary didn't actually screw him, but would have loved to have done. She thought she was in with a chance but then found him (Paul) with one of his administrative staff sitting on his knee, after a college function. Mary was really jealous of the new woman in his life, whom he later left his wife for and married. She (Mary) then took up with another member of staff (Mark) who was employed on a lower status grade on the next level of management. Mary has a powerful position in the senior management team. Mark had been married for the third time. In fact he and one of his wives had swapped partners with their best friends and apparently they still see each other as a foursome. Anyway, Mary set out to get him and got him — he left his wife. Mary stopped dying her hair as Mark was much older than her and let it grow naturally grey, which fascinated me; I felt he'd probably liked her because she obviously was younger! Mary and Mark were a very strong team together. They convinced the Principal of a new college management structure. She had vision and so the college was reorganised. Mark now became one of three second-layer managers. Mary, Mark and Paul were now peers. **(see Fig. 1)**

CASE STUDIES

Figure 1. Management hierarchy

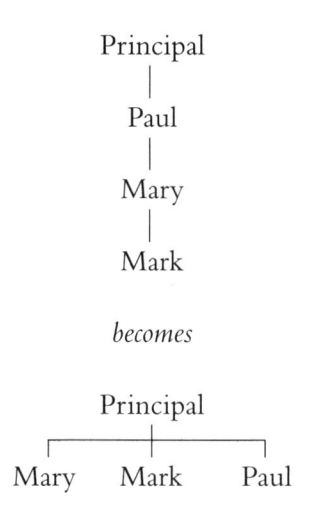

Principal
|
Paul
|
Mary
|
Mark

becomes

Principal
|
Mary   Mark   Paul

Mary is a Lucretia Borgia – out for herself. If you're with her you're fine, if you're not you're stuffed! I was one of the people with her. Paul ended up feeling guilty about leaving his wife and children and moved back and forward from wife to mistress. Then the Principal goes off sick and Paul becomes the Principal. Mary's lover Mark is now the Vice Principal. So Paul, got rid of Mark and one of the Heads is now upset because she liked working for Mark. In fact, she probably fancied Mark!

Paul would have loved to have done anything to get rid of Mary and Mark. Now we also have Tony, an ex-senior lecturer with me at work, who is now the male Lucretia Borgia! Mary appointed Tony and thought he was great. Tony chats up Paul, the director and he is then made a head of faculty and then later deputy director. Tony, the ex-senior lecturer with me is now above me and is now Mega director. Tony suggests a flattened management structure which knocks out Mary and Mark. Paul agrees. Mary and Mark leave with a bit of a helpful push.

CASE STUDIES

Future connections

Then I moved the interview into the future stage. 'Having talked about your past and your present, have you made any connections that might affect you in the future?'

Yes, I am so unlike my mother, a woman always at home. I think my brother is what my parents would have wanted and expected him to be. Not me. I've got some of my father's strengths and character but I'm very unlike my mother who lacks confidence. She finds it hard to be confident and thinks I'm wrong to be so confident and pushy. I went away to university, which helped.

Vivienne then changed her tone in a light hearted, relaxed one to reveal a sadness as she relived her memories. 'All my friends at 11 passed the eleven-plus. I didn't! I was absolutely devastated that all my friends went to the grammar school and I didn't.' She switched emotions. She smiled. 'But, I ended up on top as Head Girl, games captain and prefect. Got all my O levels although my friends didn't; then I went to university and they didn't. I was built up at secondary school. My confidence came from there.' She celebrated her achievement but switched again to looking and sounding sad as she continued the story.

My father died the month I was going to university so I went the year after. Once I got there my confidence was knocked. Compared with the other students, I realised I was pretty thick. I was not the best any more, but very lucky. I regret the way I reacted to university life because I had a boyfriend throughout and didn't use the university as I should have done. It's the biggest regret of my life, wasting time whilst I was there, not enjoying university life to the full. It's a unique time and experience and I wasted it to a great extent.

CASE STUDIES

As far as the future is concerned if I thought I wasn't attractive I'd lack confidence. I hope I'll become an attractive person rather than only attractive sexually. In fact I'd love to be like you. You're both physically attractive with a charismatic personality. I've no confidence, I'm not charismatic, only physically attractive. I dress to look attractive but I want them (men) to think I look nice, not sexy. If they said I looked sexy I'd go home and take it off. I still like the director but it was nasty and unforgivable what he did to the others, but I like them all!

Analysis

Vivienne was still influenced by her early sexual message, wanting to look nice not sexy. As she said, she would go home and change her dress if she thought she looked sexy. The organizational story, meanwhile, bears out Martin's analysis of one of the commonest stories told; 'Look how someone of a high status behaved so badly!'

Vivienne also demonstrates aspects of sex roles as discussed in Chapter 2 which are highlighted as she 'gets away' with certain behaviour because she is a woman.

★ ★

3. Steve – swinging Sixties scene

Steve's eyes twinkled throughout most of the first three-quarters of the interview. His humour was contagious; his laughter came deep from within a large muscular shell. I found the interview warm, passionate and genuine.

Early sexual experiences

'What were your early sexual experiences, Steve?'

'It was happening to everyone in the swinging Sixties, except me!

'I was a virgin until I was 22,' he began. On being asked about childhood experiences Steve described his early years. 'I was told nothing about sex, but it was commented on, through humour. My father never really talked much to us throughout all our lives.'

Then there was a lowering of his head and a sinking of his eyes as he added, 'After my mother died I became very close to my sister and she always used to say,' now he was lifting up his smiling face again, '"Don't go out without your wellies on" referring to condoms.' He laughed heartily.

Steve's first sexual experience was in his early twenties, in London. He reasoned that this was because he was engaged to a devout Roman Catholic. As he recalled this time in his life, he spoke as if he were being strangled, not wanting to feel or explore his emotions about these years. In talking about the experience he said 'it was all right!' but it sounded to me as though it wasn't all right but as much as could be expected for a first-time sexual penetrative experience.

I asked him about his sexual orientation. He squared his shoulders, put his arms symmetrically around his chest, having had one of his arms along the back of the settee, and said 'I'm heterosexual all right but I have a problem with homosexuality, in terms of accepting it.' His humour took over: 'I still have a problem – but I don't move my body now – I've been on a Jeanie Civil course!'

Present sexuality
We moved on to explore the area of sexuality at work. I focused on what happened to Steve at work and in what ways he felt that his sexuality affected him.

'Well, it affects me in interviews. I always believed in the truism not to appoint people you don't like, and if I like them, then there is a sexual link.' Steve told me several stories about sexuality at work, the first being about his own affairs with two female members of staff. One was a member of the support staff and the other was the first appointment that he had made years earlier. He recalled these with pleasure; they had both been pleasant, seemingly leaving no scars of guilt but now a slight show of embarrassment as he was telling me. This reminded me of interviewing someone else in the medical profession who revealed a similar power relationship with a member of staff. Having told me his story in detail, he then looked at me and said 'Are you cross with me?' Maybe he was looking for my approval, or he needed reassurance that what he had revealed was in keeping with other stories and that his story was not unique.

Then Steve went on to tell me about a relationship he had had with a student.

We were all on this field trip, sleeping in tents and we all went down to the pub. I suppose I must have had about ten pints otherwise I wouldn't have fancied her. Well, actually I didn't. I remember it was when the group were walking back from the pub that I gave her this innocuous cuddle, and as we walked up the hill I thought nothing of it but when I got back to my tent she was lying in my bed, naked.

He went on to talk about how embarrassing it had been the next morning because all the students knew: 'Anyway, it was the end of term and I was really glad to see the back of them.' Unfortunately he had love bites on his neck which he explained away as catching himself on the branches of a tree, and those bites that could be seen he cut with a razor in order to create an explanation for his wife.

All this had been in Steve's earlier career but he updated his response to how his sexuality affects him now. He is having an affair with another member of the senior management team. Steve's sexuality affected him positively at work. He smiled and said 'because I work in the presence of someone I like a lot, it affects me positively. It makes it pleasant to be at work. Meaningful relationships enhance positive characteristics you have,' he philosophised. Then he added

'There are no negative aspects at work as our relationship grew out of deep friendship.' I enquired about the aspect of confidentiality, with regard to the working environment but Steve thought that this was not a problem. 'No, if people say "Don't discuss this with Mary", I don't. There are things about work that I would not discuss with her and things she does not discuss with me.'

He continued with his sexual stories about the organization. 'A senior inspector came up to me and said "I hear there is an interesting relationship in the senior management team!" I thought "Oh shit, she's found out about me", but it wasn't me he had been told about; it was the director who was bringing a man in from another college to take a senior management position. This always generates rumour, founded or unfounded.'

'The director jumps on him at meetings,' Steve continued, as he painted the picture for me of his principal and his chosen colleague. In transactional analysis terms, he operates from Parent to Child always when he speaks to him.'

Some time later after this interview Steve added to his story of the director and his rumoured liaison with the other member of the management team, informing me of the new management strategy and reorganization of the team which would now include a man with whom he was having a sexual liaison. This created a good deal of anguish for another member of the team because he felt undermined by the new line manager. Nobody considers that men may also be appointed to senior positions because of their sexual liaisons.

I asked him about organizational sexual messages and Steve offered two. One message was that 'You don't need to be a man to get on in this place as a large percentage of senior management team are female' and the second message was 'There is an unwritten law – don't do it with students.'

He laughed as he crossed his legs and leaned forward supporting his head in his hand as I asked him how often sexuality affected him at work. 'Not very often but I think I suffer from sexuality at work because the Principal has a better relationship with the women on the senior management team than the men on it, so I suffer as a man on that team.

Steve's lightness left him temporarily as he talked about others. 'There seem to be more broken marriages these days. I think it is the extra work – hence working patterns are longer. But some like it. Perhaps it is a way of avoiding partners when the relationship is not so good. Or it could be that it is more common maybe in my age group.' Steve then referred to several people we both knew who had experienced or were presently going through the trauma of breaking up their marriages.

> *I'm in life crisis stuff. I now have to work from eight to six. I have to work harder to survive. People share their problems with me. I support staff. I have more empathy with women at work. The other evening I was genuinely working late. I telephoned home and got a frosty reaction – so I said angrily I could be standing here in a pool of blood.*

I challenged him at this point as to how honest he was being and he replied 'OK, a bit of me was not wanting to go home.' He concluded the interview by adding:

> *Another evening I didn't get home until ten o'clock. My wife wanted to talk about our relationship. I wasn't interested; you know, 'the lights are on but nobody's in'. On the other hand, Mary picks up on thoughts just like that*

he concluded, happily snapping his fingers and smiling.

Future outcomes

Although Steve is energised by his sexuality at work, he is contemplating leaving both his job and his wife in order to feel free of the pressures of his relationships at work and allow space for his lover to make a decision about her future, either to stay with him or her husband.

Analysis

Steve's early recalled experience was that sex was talked about via humour and he certainly exhibited that early manner in the interview. The organizational message of 'not with students' was borne out in his sexual story of a bad sexual involvement with a student. Steve suggested that keeping confidences might prove difficult when he recalled the anxieties about keeping or breaking confidential information when two senior managers are involved in a sexual relationship.

I think sexuality affects Steve at work more than 'not very often' as his involvement with his senior manager suggests. Also he experiences difficulties in relating to his Principal because he gets on with women better than Steve.

Steve displayed wanting to be seen as macho when asked about homosexuality. He also told the story of 'rule breaking by a high status person' – the director – and how sexuality has a positive effect on him at work.

★ ★

4. Pru-prudish passion

Pru is tall, slim, sensuous, smartly dressed with all matching accessories. She has a bright, lively, energetic voice, speaking quickly and being specific in her responses. Her stories are told poignantly, succinctly but with a touch of critical analysis about her as she unfolds the layers of her sexuality at work.

Early sexual experiences

'My mother never told me anything about sex and my father never talked about it either,' was her reply to my question about her early sexual messages. She added: 'really, the message was be prudish.'

'What was your first sexual experience?' I enquired.

'I felt let down really, despite going out with this boyfriend for four years. It was in the scout hall. He was a venture scout and he had kept the key for the scout hut. I was nearly 17 and he was at university, that was my first time when penetration happened.' She smiled happily as she said 'Mentally, I'm no different now to when I was 16.' Then she reminisced about her relationship. 'We used to say that we'd get married, but we did not really mean it. I'd do my pottery and he'd write on a Scottish island where we would live.'

Pru shared her sexual orientation with me as being heterosexual 'No, I have never been with a woman. I shared a flat with a gay man. We were really close friends. I can cope with it in men but I'm not good at coping with it in women.'

Present sexual experience

'What about now? Do you still carry those messages today; are you still prudish now?' I ventured.

'No. John (the man in her life for two years) 'made me feel very different. For the first time in my life I feel very comfortable and very open about my sexuality. It's so brilliant! I have been totally open right from the beginning with him.' This response was very strongly and positively delivered.

'What did he do to make you feel that way?' I asked.

'It's comfortable but still exciting and passionate. He bought this book on sexual ecstasy and said that he wanted to achieve it with me and I said to him "How will you know when we've got it because I feel that anyway now!" I have everything on equal terms: he's good at feeling the temperature, I feel security and respect and have absolute confidence in him.' She was delighted and energised. This positive construction later changed in the projection stage.

'What about work – does your sexuality affect you in anyway at work?' I asked, moving into a new area.

I don't think so, as I came from industry and we changed together. I was always the only woman working with all men as their duty manager. Also I was only one of the very few female students with men at college and my students are mainly male. Sometimes I'm a bit prudish and don't understand what's going on.

Pru continued with the subject of dress. She spoke explicitly. 'I tend to be very conservative; I don't think it's appropriate to wear sexual clothes at work. I do wear attractive clothes outside. At work I would never wear short skirts, as I have thin legs – just suits. I suppose it means I'm prudish.'

Pru moved away from the aspect of dress as she swung her thinking around to her managing director. 'He has a problem with clever women. I avoid him if I can. I don't think he finds me very easy to deal with.' I think at this point there was a tacit statement of her intelligence. She continued 'Don't think he finds women easy to deal with. He's OK with the ones that he's able to think for. If you go with an opinion to treat men differently from women, he doesn't take women seriously.'

'What are your sexual stories about work, Pru?' I enquired.

Well, Ted, the deputy director, and I worked together. When we started our relationship I didn't want it to be an affair, it would have made it sordid, so one of us had to leave as we couldn't have developed the relationship. Once we knew he was going things changed.

The previous director had many 'friends'. In fact, three at one time. He was well known for chatting up the women. We used to have to signal to each other through the door to be helped out by other staff, if you were on your own in a room with him. Two of his senior management team are together as well.

'What are the sexual messages in the organization?'

'If it's OK from the top. Let's have a field day! But I'm not sure about this.' She answered quickly as if she had said this many times before her relationship with Ted. 'People used to put in long hours and relationships developed. Now they just do their hours and go home.'

Future connections

'Having reflected on these questions have you made any links with the past and the present?' She nodded 'And in what ways might this affect you in the future at work?' I continued.

'Things shock me and I can't say anything. Bad language, I can't cope with it.' I was reminded of her prudish messages again, as she went on:

Like Barclays Banker (meaning wanker). I didn't know what the word meant anyway. I realise now I could never have had a 'hole in the corner' affair with Ted and we never declared it because of the director. I was once playing tennis with Ted before our relationship developed and I said to someone, joking, 'Don't tell my husband'. The incident was then passed around the office where there is a hotbed of gossip.

Pru paused. I remained silent as she gathered her thoughts then continued:

The main thing for me is that I will age anyway and I will be seen less and less in that way. I don't need to hide in the same way as I'm now seen as a person with a brain not a body with a brain. My relationship with Ted has made me more confident.'

Again she stopped speaking momentarily and then continued emphatically and in a louder voice to the one that she had been using up until that moment.

> *Above all I've now realised that my ex-husband, Philip, gave me the same message as my mother which was you can't work and have children. When I work at the weekends now Ted looks after the children and he's great. Ted now treats me as an equal so I foresee myself becoming more confident about the future now I've made those links.*

Her body relaxed a little but her face remained intense as she spoke.

> *Philip was not like my dad at all. Ted is. I now realise the link with marrying my father. There's only ever been two people in my life that I've felt comfortable with and only two people for whom I have confidence and total respect, my dad and Ted. Dad's reserved; so is Ted, and they are both very tall. Any man that has been special to me has been very tall, six foot three inches and above.*

She smiled and leaned back on the stiff upright chair, her posture mirroring the furniture.

Analysis

Pru had made connections between her early childhood and adulthood. At the end of the interview she was more relaxed and smiled more often as some of her tension lifted. Her projection of her future at work was positive [50]. Her confessional tale led her to make important links for herself. Pru's language was prudish throughout, she never admitted in such words that she was sexually intimate with Ted. She always referred to her relationship developing. She spoke of the director's friends rather than lovers, two of the senior managers being together rather than cohabiting. Possibly enforcing her prudish early messages, she referred to 'bad language, and it seems her sex role messages had been 'You can't work and have children' but she broke from that role and is now more able to operate in her career as a manager, with her new partner treating her as an equal not as a subservient woman.

She made the links with her father and her new partner, recognising some comfort within that relationship demonstrating the Jungian concept of Shadowing [50]. Her references to how she dressed support Kanter's [15] findings and the stereotyping of sex roles endorses Shakeshaft's work [48]. A year later Pru was still with Ted but was still wondering whether to commit herself to marriage as her career was now very rewarding and giving her a great deal of job satisfaction.

★ ★

5. Andy – angry and aware

Andy is tall, slim, serious looking, with a warm smile and deep laugh that happens infrequently, as we work through the interview. He is intelligent, quick thinking, makes psychological connections quickly because of his academic background and knowledge of the subject. I set out the ground rules for the interview as previously described under the first interview 'Nick'.

Early sexual experiences

'What are your early sexual messages, Andy?' I began.

'I didn't think I had any but there was something I've been told.' He started to tell his story.

> *When I was very small, about two or three years old, I lived in a flat and was taken outside by a little girl, who was about four, to give me a 'blow job' then wanted me to do the same to her, but she had*

> *nothing to suck. I remember her name was Judy and so I had conflicting messages. My mother came round the corner of the garage and took me away. She was angry and/or embarrassed. I think she was afraid someone would see us.*

'What would you say was your first sexual experience that you can recall, rather than having been told about it?'

'When I was three I may have been abused by my aunt. I am pretty sure that some woman used me to masturbate her.' Andy looked angry again. 'There is a lot of anger connected with that,' he added.

Present sexuality

'Now what are your present attitudes about sexuality?' I asked. He replied quietly, his tone was sombre as he started to reply but changed as he continued his story.

> *I don't know where I am. I'm a very sexual person and I have just gone through a big re-evaluation. I want to have a full relationship with one woman. I hope that can be my wife. It's not happening now; sex has become so painful. No room for me to be in it any longer. I am supposed to have an erection on demand about every one and half months. I become angry and I lose my erection. I feel as though she has managed my sexuality. The only way I can handle it is by being solidly where I am. I can move myself. My first work is on me.*

He looked angry as he spoke in a resentful way about his wife.

'Are you sublimating?' I enquired.

> *I practise a form of meditation which circulates sexual energy throughout the body, pulling it up the spine and drawing it down across the face, neck, chest and abdomen. Is that sublimation? I smiled as his question went unanswered.*

'How would you describe your sexual orientation?'

'Heterosexual. Homosexuality makes me feel yukky. It feels predatory and infantile.'

'What are your sexual stories at work?'

There was a period when I slept with many women staff and students, and colleagues of mine. I remember being in a classroom with some students that I'd slept with and the dynamics of that. My sexuality was all over the place but it didn't seem to make any difference. I never felt blackmailed into giving people extra marks. Thinking about it now I don't think anyone was after that either.

I taught in Cambridge when I was 31. This woman offered me a job. The next year she offered me the job again and I accepted it and then she passed me off as her toy boy. I played into it. I'm sure I knew I was using my sexuality but I would have denied it then. It was another teacher who I was having a sexual relationship with who pointed it out to me. I remember I was surprised at the time.'

Andy paused, put his hands around his head and blurted out.

Oh God, this is such a gross memory. My supervisor is 60, a dynamic and energetic woman. I love her to death. We were driving back from Birmingham late one night we had talked about why there were no men in her life. I remember saying to her if I was 50 years old, I'd be after you like a shot.

'Does your sexuality affect you at work now?' I asked as Andy was making his connections of thought.

> *In the prison I don't use it. I do have sexual feelings for some members of staff though but I don't act on them. That is, other than to note them and enjoy them. I'm not after anything now.*

'What about sexual stories about others at work?' I continued.

> *Well, one story is that the prison governor slept with his secretary in his office on his desk. She is now married to one of the officers.*

Future outcomes

'Thinking about early messages and present situations, have you made any connections with them? In the future, what might change for you now?'

> *I need to give myself permission and allow myself to feel sexual. I hung on to my sexuality because I was scared of being promiscuous. I will control my behaviour but I need not control my feelings. I could be this great big, juicy man!*

As the interview closed I said 'I am thinking, Andy, that there was anger. First when you were used to masturbate some girl, and anger now with your wife. You implied that both women had power over you. I suggest that you might want to think about that.'

'No,' he said 'I don't want to think about it, but I will. I think you're probably right. Thanks,' he smiled and nodded as we said our goodbyes holding hands. His eyes were clear and his brow was unfurrowed.

Analysis

Andy had been working on getting in touch with his feelings and seemed to have arrived, for he is now contemplating some new behaviour. He was addressing the issue of women having sexual power over him and had made a connection with anger and power. Andy demonstrated how people can change their attitudes by giving themselves permission. He also showed how he worked through his cognitive, affective and behavioural stages of attitude formation [24].

Meeting me some six months later he was far more at peace with himself, less aggressive and did not feel that he had to control his feelings as he had been doing. He now felt 'juicy'. There were still, however, sexual difficulties with his wife.

★ ★

6 Fiona – father couldn't be nearer

Fiona was small, with mid-length, animated hair, her face moved expressively as she told her story. Her eyes reflected her happiness and sadness alternately as she first recalled her father's messages about sexuality.

Early sexual experiences

'Dad put me on a Grecian pedestal. I felt ugly and fat on it.' She slumped as if she was recalling how it felt to me on this pedestal as she talked to me. 'He (father) used to say "No man will want you if you get off the pedestal, and never get off it until you are married."' Fiona continued to tell me about her father: how he hated coquettishness and how she never felt loved by him, although her mother told her how much her father did love her. 'Neither of my parents talked to me about sexuality. I never saw anybody naked. I remember asking my mother about sexuality, and she gave me this book about rabbits. When I started my periods at 14. Mother just said 'there are some sanitary towels at the bottom of the airing cupboard'. Fiona then went on to talk about her early sexual experiences.

'My first sexual experience was when I was 15, at a party. This boy put his hands on my breast and gave me a French kiss. I rejected his further moves and it went all round the school that I was frigid, because the boys were all mates.' She appeared sad as she continued with the story of her early relationships. 'I was brought up as a Roman Catholic. I was confused about my sexuality, and sex before marriage was certainly not on.' This seemed to fit with her father's message not to get off the pedestal until you are married. 'At 15 I had a Jewish, Communist boyfriend but he was never allowed in our house. I was 20 when I had my first sexual experience with a boyfriend but it was only heavy petting as I could hear my father saying "Don't get off your pedestal". Afterwards I felt ugly and fat.'

Fiona sighed heavily as she then talked about marrying her first husband Ted. 'I did not sleep with him until we were married.' She briefly told me of her marriage to this top academic at one of the two major universities where she was the little wife. Her husband was an 'expert' professor of sociology and lectured on the inequalities of people, but not at home. 'At home, I just entertained at the table with all these big names sitting there.' She left him, taking her children with her. This was the only reference she made to her children.

Present sexuality

We reflected on sexual orientation. 'I am heterosexual but I have been propositioned by a number of women to have a relationship but I haven't experimented.' She added 'Although I am not very interested in men now really.' She then began reconstructing the past again. 'There have only been four men in my life.'

After she had left Ted she met Mark, 'It was a head affair at first – he understood my insecurities and took me seriously. We had a passionate affair. I was his little plaything. He said I was beautiful.' She looked relieved as she added 'Mark left me and I am now married to Roy. He is younger than me, and it's more a problem for me than it is for him, our age difference.' She smiled and looked happy as she mentioned Roy.

Fiona then turned her attention to reflecting on how her sexuality affected her at work.

My sexuality has always been a problem for me at work. I'm a feminist. I have worked a lot with Women's Aid. When people have said 'You are very attractive' I always thought 'If you only knew!'

'What about sexual stories at work?'

Well, it is rumoured that the boss has a relationship with one of the junior members of staff, but the main story that is most commonly told is that of the advertising manager, Stuart, who is very beautiful. He has been sexually involved with numerous women at work. He suggested that we should get together. I refused. There is one man at work that I am very attracted to. His name is Howard.

Fiona continued, appearing not to give Stuart any more thinking time. 'We were friends. We had a good relationship and were close until. . .' she paused as she seemed to search for a reason, 'I was promoted and then the closeness went. He has never really spoken to me since.' She paused again and then added 'He said "You've got the job, you're stuck with it, honey".' Her face saddened and her eyes watered over.

'I remember' she continued 'when I got the job the boss said to me "Your getting the job was quite a surprise to me." I thought how hard we have to work to be seen. (We being Fiona) Sometimes I think I'm invisible.' Her face tensed. 'Howard and I were such good friends. We went on holiday in a foursome. We had lots of fun!' Fiona smiled as she recalled the good times. Her expression changed as she added, 'His wife left him and we used to joke about having an affair.'

Future connections

Suddenly Fiona stiffened, and her eyes filled with tears as she experienced an 'ah ah' (that is when a connection is made and the person makes some sense of what they are thinking or feeling) and reflected on her own sexual story. She then theorised.

'I've just realised – Howard is like my father and like Ted – critical, taking his bat and ball away and not talking, leaving me feeling powerless. Howard doesn't say he values me; neither did my father or Ted.' She concluded with 'I'm going to change the habit of a lifetime. 'I'm going to talk to him.'

Analysis

Having waited until she was married to have sex Fiona could now get down from her pedestal. When she talked about four men in her life I later realised that one of these four men was in fact her father, as she had only had three male lovers. When Fiona made the connection that Howard was like her father and like Ted, this was an important realisation for her. This follows the idea of how people can react to psychological shadows and may project on to individuals other people's behaviour or attitudes. This can be both positive and negative. The fact that Fiona was going to talk to Howard rather than avoid doing so, which had been her previous pattern of behaviour, was a positive step towards recognising her own self-worth.

★ ★

7. Paul – positively promoted

Paul is tall, slim and lively. He moves his arms, shoulders and legs frequently as he communicates. He talks quickly and openly about his lifestyle. As he recalled different times in his life there was laughter in his voice. Life for Paul was about having fun. He lives with a partner. He works in the computing industry and as he described his work he emphasised how much he enjoyed it and that he was good at his job. Paul brought a great deal of energy and light-heartedness to the interview.

Early sexual experiences
'What were your early messages about sexuality, Paul?' I began.

'Very little really. I cannot recall sex being discussed really, though I do remember being given a pamphlet and told I could ask my mum questions and she would always answer them. My dad died when I was three months old so I have no memories of him.'

'What is your attitude to sex now?' I continued.

He quickly replied, 'I like it, and plenty of it. I am open about my sexuality. I do not hide the fact that I am gay. I'm still enquiring about sex and I like to be adventurous with it. The more the merrier.'

I went on to ask about his first sexual experience.

'I suppose my first sexual experience that I remember was at school. I would be about four and I was looking at other boys – I never looked at the girls in that way. From a very young age I knew I was gay. I would just stand looking at them.'

Present sexuality
When I enquired about the sexual messages at work Paul wanted to know what I meant. 'Give me a clue of the sort of things that you mean.'

I answered with 'I don't want to influence your answer really by saying too much, but the sort of things that are said or not said about people's sexuality. Messages can be spoken or unspoken. It's what you pick up.'

'Right, I see what you mean. Yes, they are open, tolerant and accommodating. I think there is positive discrimination on being openly gay. I have certainly been promoted as a result of being gay. It's like, he's doing a reasonable job and he's gay too. I think some of the staff have a covert feeling about being gay.'

Again, he was quick to reply and had no hesitation about the messages, and this openness continued as he responded to the enquiry about his sexuality at work.

'I have a very busy social life outside work, so I don't socialise with people at work. I think because I am open about my sexuality, people can talk to me easily. There is a girl in the office with lesbian tendencies and she finds me someone she can open up to. Other people talk candidly about sex. It's a fairly young organization, so people can talk about anything. Sex, drugs – you name it, we talk about it. No one seems to take offence. I am sure I could go in and say I had my arse spanked last night and no one would blink an eyelid.' He laughed at the thought.

I went on to ask 'What about sexual stories at work, do people talk about other people's sexuality?'

'Yes, there are loads. One of the project managers got off with one of the customers. That caused a bit of tale telling. Then there are different staff who have had it off with other staff. It's happening all the time.'

Finally, I asked Paul if his sexuality affected him at work.

'Everything affects me at work, not just my sexuality. Yes, being gay certainly affects me at work and being *me* affects me.' He emphasised 'My sexuality affects me in a positive way. I've always known I was gay and I've never been with a woman, not even to experiment. Oh! I've just remembered, when I was little I didn't like football.'

The interview finished. I thanked him for his openness and frankness and asked him if I could write his story as a case history. He said that he was pleased to have been selected.

I arranged to send him the copy of the interview as I did with all the other case studies, and that if anything seemed untrue, misinterpreted or threatening, then he could feel free to comment on it. Even though names and places are changed to maintain confidentiality, it would only be published with his permission.

Analysis

Paul's early memories of little being said, but that questions were always answered by his mother, seemed to have influenced him in that he also answered questions quickly and comfortably. He used only a few words to come quickly to the point. His openness was refreshing and his comments about everything affecting him positively demonstrated his positive self-image, unlike so many interviewees who were still struggling to break free from sexual taboos and early abuse.

★ ★

8. Hilary – horrible to happy

Hilary was animated, lively, smiled widely and had clear blue eyes that twinkled and danced. Some of the time she looked distanced, hurt or angry by some of her recollections. Most of the time her body language looked earthed, she spoke in an empowered way and gave off a warmth that was comfortable and trusting.

Early sexual experiences

'What was your early sexual message, Hilary?'

'Well, I suppose it was: sex is something you don't talk about, especially if you are a girl. My mother used to say "naughty girl" if I ever showed my knickers or walked about with a bare bottom. "Cover yourself up, nobody wants to look at your rudies." I can hear her now and see her wagging finger and screwed-up nose. Sometimes she slapped my hands, not hard, if I was playing with myself. She used to say "We really wanted a boy when we had you, but you'll do".'

'What were your early sexual experiences?' I went on to ask.

Horrible, horrible. I am shuddering just remembering. I have been for counselling with three different people. I've been in therapy for a year now. I've already worked on my childhood stuff but bits of baggage still keep popping up, even now. When I was three or four I was with my dad's brother, I don't like calling him uncle because that seems to attach me and I want to sever the links mentally and physically. He was weird. I mean he was complex, because he could be so nice to me in front of others and then just change into a Hyde character when we were on our own. This was a highly respectable man of society, local councillor, social worker and church-goer. He was married, I say was because he has been divorced twice — so much for his church pontifications! He was slimy. I've thought about why lots of times but the only answer I've come up with is that with paedophiles it must be inherent.

He came to stay with us one Easter with his two kids. His wife wasn't with him. I learned years later that she had left him and taken her daughter with her. At first it was fun because he took me out with his sons and we went to the seaside and went on to the funfair. It was good going with lads because they were a bit more daring than some of my silly scared little friends. Then when we got back the lads slept in my room on the floor on some mattress, cushion things I think, and he came in. I feel so stupid thinking about it now because he was babysitting and said to come into his bed because there was more room. I went, I remember, taking this furry donkey with me. It was horrible. He hurt me. He said we were having secret donkey rides just like on the sands and I would love it but to keep quiet because he only wanted to give me a special donkey ride, not the boys. He called his penis his donkey's tail and put it in my mouth. I feel as though I am choking as I'm telling you this.

Anyway, the rest is the usual guilt stuff: "our secret, no-one will believe you, you're special" and other heavy bollocks. I never did say anything because just a little bit of me liked it, but I remember saying I didn't want him to babysit when he came again, without his boys. I think my mother knew all along, although she died before I could ask her 20 years later when I dealt with the rubbish.

CASE STUDIES

Family stories talk about his first wife who found him in bed with their daughter. Then he had two step-daughters in his second marriage and rumour is rife that it happened again. I feel angry that my mother or dad let that happen to me. She (mother) should have known and he (dad) should have protected me from him. He must have known. A brother surely must know. They used to sleep together in a double bed as kids.

Hilary stopped, tears ran down her face, and we sat silently. She continued, 'God, you would think after all these years I'd be over it, wouldn't you?' I asked if she would like to stop the interview but she said, 'No, let's go on, it may help to work through and resolve something.'

Present sexual experiences

'What about now? What is your attitude to sex?' I enquired, watching her face as she appeared to recall and remember those early days.

'Oh, no problem. I love sex and I talk freely to my six-year-old about sex and love. She's called Lucy.'

'So your early messages not to talk about sexuality have changed,' I responded.

'Yes, but it's taken a lot of work to get to this stage.' she replied.

'Does your sexuality affect you at work, Hilary?'

I manage a staff of 18 and there is one man who is gay. I only found out because he is a friend of someone I know socially. When I told him I knew his friend I think he realised I knew about him. Once or twice he nearly seemed to be going to say something, but stopped. We were on a residential conference and we were both a bit tiddly but we didn't. I expect it's for the best.

There is still so much prejudice about. There was just one woman, who has now left the firm, that I had a one night stand with. It was OK, although she was bisexual, and I wondered if it (a heterosexual liaison) had been something she just wanted to experiment with. She was going for promotion and I would have been on the interviewing panel. That would have been difficult for me because I would have favoured her because she was good, not just because I'd fucked her. I suppose my sexuality affects me at work in that I cannot be open about my present partner. It's Christmas parties and all that that get difficult. In fact, I got my brother's mate to come with me last year because it was the first Christmas after my divorce. It's funny you know, two women living together is thought of as natural — you know, two little homemakers — yet two men sharing and most people are suspicious that they are gay.

Future connections

'You've talked about your sexuality as a child and how your are affected at work. Have you made any connections?'

Yes. My boss calls me Hils; my husband used to call me that. We were good mates. He was more like a brother. Kindly, good at the old DIY, but sexually there was nothing. He didn't have much of a sex drive and I met my present partner at pre-school playgroup with all the other mums. We just connected. It started with coffees and then one day we had some wine and it happened. It was, and still is, just wonderful. She makes me feel happy and replete.

I think I've always known, although occasionally I do see a man I find attractive, but it's not the same physical throb. She (Jane) is like me. It's like talking to myself, being with her. Jane had a bad start, she was interfered with in a residential home. Nobody believed her. I've just realised how similar our experiences are. We both left nice husbands. God, there was a scandal. We moved here a year ago to make a fresh start. The neighbours think we're two divorcees helping each other financially to get a home and look after the kids. I've just remembered the "wanted a boy" message and that's why they called me Hilary. Dad said, "we were going to call you Hilary or Leslie if you were a boy, but you could still have that name." Fancy not realising that before!

I've also just realised that I don't like one of my staff because he has the same name and beard as my dad's brother. I knew there was something about him. It makes sense now. That's a bit unfair of me as a manager, isn't it?

The interview finished with Hilary deciding to look at her behaviour towards her uncle's namesake.

Analysis

Hilary made connections and had moved from feeling negative to positive about her sexuality. She demonstrated a managerial fairness about her relationships with her staff and was concerned to find that her behaviour was negative towards one of her staff simply on the basis of a name.

Hilary highlights the difficulty that many gay managers experience in not being able to be honest about their gayness for fear of repercussions.

★ ★

9. Bryan – beauty and the beast

Bryan is very tall, slim and blonde. He is long-armed and long-legged. He is mostly bald with fair hair at the sides of his face and the lower back head. He moves and winds his arms and legs about him as he talks. He looked pensive and serious for the majority of the interview but occasionally he would smile broadly and his eyes would dance mischievously.

CASE STUDIES

Early sexual experiences

'What were your early messages about sex or sexuality, Bryan?' I began.

They were neutral messages. I don't recall any strong messages. I had the usual sexual stereotypes that men were men and very negative messages about deviating from being a normal heterosexual. I am an only child so I didn't get any female messages from sisters. My mother seemed to say, without actually saying it, that it was a taboo subject really. My father died when I was three, so I don't remember much about him, only what I have been told. My mother said look for beauty in people. Sex really was something to be hidden and secret.

'Is that your attitude now?'

Not really, but I'm not bothered by sex so much now. I mean I'm not so interested in actual sexual intercourse and scoring with either sex — more in relationships. Men and women fascinate me. I've learned to let out my feminine side and don't feel so threatened now when I express feelings. I've always thought that I was a bit stupid intellectually, but now I realise that other people feel the same. It may be the same with sex. I've always thought that my sexuality brought out the beast in me. There is another side to me I don't like.

You know when you are told that sex is dirty, rude, or it's a taboo subject, and you like it, you get very mixed up. Worse than that, I went against the norm. I wanted sex with men and women. I still do, although I have more mental sex now. AIDS and all that has frightened me. In my twenties I jumped from one to the other and played the field. Now I can't keep up the pace with everything else going on at home and at work, and I'm getting older and less fit these days. My physical attractiveness is diminishing. Some say that you get more interesting as you get older, but I think your sex drive goes off pretty rapidly after 40.

CASE STUDIES

That was a long answer, wasn't it? I do tend to go on a bit! What was the question again?

'What is your attitude now to sex and sexuality?'

'. . . I am not bothered by sex particularly, that is, regular intercourse. I'm more interested in the more subtle sexual interrelations between people. I don't think I'm scared of sex but I am unwilling to upturn my life by inviting new sexual partners of both sexes now.'

'What about your first sexual experience, Bryan?' I asked.

It is difficult to recall which was the first because sexuality was always with me as far back as I can remember. There was playing with other girls and boys in the back entry (a place, not anatomically). There was mutual masturbation in the gym behind the horse. Once we were nearly discovered, me and Robertson. Froggart (a teacher) came in and obviously heard us. Fortunately he said "Is someone hiding in here?" which gave us time to readjust ourselves and give the excuse for being there that yes, we were hiding.

I've read a lot about homosexuality because there was a time when I thought I was gay. That wasn't the word in my day: queer, poof, shit-shover, come to mind. Most people seem to have had traumatic beginnings of abuse, but I don't remember anything incestuous, or being taken against my will. I like it. I liked the feeling. I believe virtually all little boys play with each other. We certainly did at public school, but then there were no girls. I'm not sure if I had been in a mixed school I would have had the same inclinations, although I think everybody is bisexual to some degree.

I really fancied my woodwork master. He had this tight arse and I used to play with myself when he was bending down or leaning over a bench showing some kid some skill or other. I remember the games with girls and boys, in the hols, that grew into kissing games and dare games. "You show me yours and I'll show you mine." My first penetrative sex was at 15 with a girl from our road called Freda but it grew from all the fumblings and trying it on from between 12 and 15. I also tried sodomy at about the same age with this guy at school but it didn't work. I think I was a bit worried about what was up there so it put me off and I lost my erection. In later years as I became more biologically aware I did have anal sex with a fellow scout on summer camp. Anal sex is something I have always enjoyed with both sexes.

Present sexual experiences

'So how would you describe your sexual orientation: homosexual, bisexual, heterosexual or autosexual?' I continued.

'What do you mean, autosexual?' Bryan look puzzled.

'Sexually satisfying yourself, not interested in having sex with either gender. It is a word that one of my interviewees used, but it is not in the dictionary. Some people have found it a useful word for them,' I explained.

'Oh, well, I'm bisexual. I've leant different ways at different times in my life. My teenage years were mainly homosexual, although there were a number of women. My married years, on the whole, were heterosexual – there wasn't much free time for socialising alone in those days – and now as a divorcee I'm definitely bisexual. But as I said earlier, I'm more interested in the mind, than doing it. I like beautiful people around me."

'What are the sexual messages at work, Bryan?' I asked.

Well, being in the world of finance is a bit like having a mask on most of the time. You know what I mean. You're struggling financially and you see all these people with all their money and some of the time I get jealous of both sexes because of my own financial position. We have our own code for those women who have made it by marrying into money. Also for those men who have gone into liquidation, but some like phoenixes rise from the supposed ashes, although they usually had money stashed away elsewhere unbeknown to others.

Between ourselves, there is a joke about sexual harassment – don't touch, want to be touched, couldn't touch. We talk about customers in the same way. No subject is barred really and lots of sexual banter goes on. Some of the male messages are "I can cope, let me look after you", whilst women give off different messages to different genders. To other women they give off "We women must stick together, that's typical of men," however, to men they give off the message of "I'm not really a feminist, I'm more like one of the men. I'm with you on this". Perhaps I'm talking about me. I do that too, run with the hares and hunt with the hounds.

'What stories of sexuality at work have you?' My questions were brief as Bryan had no difficulty in talking and reminiscing about his life and work.

Well, I had an affair with a member of staff four years ago and that led to my divorce. Yes, it was with a man, but it could have been a woman. The result was the same. Nobody knew at work, or so we thought, until two years later when someone joined the firm who had known my wife. I asked her to keep quiet and she said she would, but then she told one of the customers whom she knew socially, and so it slowly got rumoured. I denied all knowledge, but now I bring my woman friend to all the office functions so I think most people thought it was my wife who was being bitchy.

I have a problem with my son though, because I can see him going the same way as his dad. Chip off the old block. I resisted sending him to public school but Clare, my wife, wanted it, mainly to have more time to do her own thing. She has said that to lots of people – that's not me blaming her. Anyway, I can see the signs and he is effeminate, unsporting, and the way he moves sometimes upsets me.

He will be giving off all the gay messages to the preying men about. I do worry about him in case he gets into the whole drug or HIV scene, as he wants to do some drama and media course. I'm prejudiced about certain professions — acting, hairdressing, the Forces, catering — but we see so much of it about now on the tele and in the papers.

There's hundreds of sexual stories about the customers but within the office over the last ten years two staff have remarried, five have either divorced or left partners. One homosexual is a great salesman but is not liked by most of the men, but the women love him! I expect because there is no sexuality between them, they are not threatened by him. Some men like working with men rather than women, but I've found that women prefer men bosses too. Unless you're gay, then things change. Men don't want to work for lesbians, but women at our place are happy to work for our gay divisional head.

'You have said that your sexuality affected you at work. In what ways are you affected as a manager?'

All the time in many ways. Certainly in interviews I choose attractive people. It would go against the Equal Opportunities Commission, but I love having attractive men and women around me. You see so much ugliness in the world. I want to work and be with beautiful people. In terms of disciplining staff I find it easier to tell men off rather than women because they still use their sexuality to make you feel special, but a lot of them are quite sickening.

One woman offered herself to me quite openly some years back. She was after promotion and saw me as a way to getting it, but on that occasion I didn't. My life at that time was good and I was in love with somebody new. My sexuality affects me in who I promote because I want to feel comfortable with my senior managers because I spend so much time with them, so I appoint attractive people. But with my middle managers, because they have to produce the goods and profit margins that give me a better salary and I don't see them so much. . . I go on ability rather than appearance. I know it's wrong but there you are. I'm being honest.

Future connections
'Have you made any connection that might help you in the future?'

'Yes. One thing is my mother's emphasis on beauty could be a reason for me wanting to have beautiful people around me. The beastly bit feels less beastly. I think I'm OK in that my sexual leanings are different from most, but I am not violent or sadistic sexually, so not really beastly. I'm quite gentle and loving, really. Thanks for that.'

We finished the interview and he asked me to reassure him that this would be totally confidential.

Analysis
Bryan was aware of how his sexuality affected him at work. He appointed and managed many of his staff for their sexual attractiveness, but also wanted staff with whom he spent less time to be competent and produce the goods. His awareness of his sexual messages seemed to help him to recognise how he thinks and feels now, although his sexuality, like his early messages, was still hidden and secret.

In contradiction to Chris, who worked hard to ensure fairness and wanted to be seen doing the right thing, Bryan didn't seem to care about policies of Equal Opportunities, although he could have been honestly voicing what many managers dare not say.

★ ★

10. Chris – cocooned and cautious
Chris has a gentle, smiling, full face, whose eyes sparkle as he talks. He has a deep quiet voice and shows concern and warmth for his

staff as a managing director of a very large furnishing retail business. The interview began.

'What were your early sexual messages, Chris?' I asked.

'I cannot remember.' He paused then continued. 'Oh, I remember father telling me to be careful what I did to girls, but that was probably in my early teens. I was sent to an all-boys boarding school when I was seven because my mum was in hospital. Everyone there was into masturbation, especially on dark winter nights.' His face coloured slightly with embarrassment. 'Most of my messages came from there, nothing from my mother. Sex wasn't discussed. It seemed to be incredibly difficult. I suppose I really knew about it from an early age, being on a farm and seeing all that happens to the animals. My uncle would explain it to me in crude terms.'

I did not delve, he seemed reluctant to be more explicit. Instead, I continued with the next question.

'What is you attitude now?'

'I'm all for it,' he said laughingly. 'I am much more liberal in my attitude to sex than my parents. I talk about it to my girls even though nobody talked to me. It's easier to talk to my two younger daughters; they talk to me more than the two older ones, although I expect their mother told them what they needed to know. I would have been too embarrassed then.'

'What was your first sexual experience?' I enquired.

'Masturbation. That would have been it,' he answered quickly and completely.

'What are the sexual messages at work?' I continued.

'Anything happening on the premises is absolutely taboo, is the strong message at work. We don't have a problem if two people meet, as long as they don't mix their private life with the business. So it is "don't mix business with pleasure". Some firms prohibit married people working at the same place, but we don't.'

In response to the sexual orientation question Chris wrinkled his forehead in puzzlement at the question, saying: 'Heterosexual.'

'What are the sexual stories at work?' I went on to ask.

'There probably are loads, but in the Director's Office we are cocooned from the stories. You cannot just walk into our office; you have to be invited in. We are just five fellows together. The secretaries are all in another general office with 70 other people, so we don't get the sexual gossip but they probably do. One of us might make the odd casual remark like 'she's stunning' but otherwise the stories are non-existent. But in the rest of the building I think it is a free and easy subject!'

'What is you own sexual story?'

'Well, that's how I met my second wife. I appointed an employment agency and they supplied her for this big store opening. I was attracted to her as soon as I saw her. She wore a lovely tartan skirt and white blouse. I asked her out for a steak and one thing led to another. Two years later we were married.'

'What about sexual stories about others at work?'

Well, in my first company I went out with the office manager's daughter two or three times. I'd forgotten about her. It's so long ago but I remember a kiss and a bit of a grope in the office lift and taking her home.

Oh yes, and then there was the story of the management trainee. He and I were graduate trainees together. He was caught screwing the same office manager's other daughter. The two daughters worked for the firm. It didn't do him any good! It certainly didn't do his career any good at all, as the manager wasn't too happy with everybody gossiping about it.

Then another story is that of another senior manager in our firm who had screwed half the women in one of our branches. That's if you believe what he said.

I smiled and said, 'Does your sexuality affect you at work?'

'No,' he said emphatically and unhesitatingly. 'It did, but not now. As the director responsible for personnel I have to be seen as strictly fair and even-handed. Any potential sexual discrimination or racist discrimination can get us now into all kinds of trouble in a big company like ours.'

My silence prompted him to elaborate.

Someone got carried away recently and their racist remark could now cost our company umpteen thousands of pounds. In general any large employer has to be scrupulously careful in the way in which they deal with people who want to join the company.

Any slight indication that someone may be of the wrong sex or wrong colour can mean that you are taken to the cleaners, if they feel that they are being unfairly treated.

'Are you saying that legislation stops you from making sexist or racist remarks?'

Chris smiled. 'If you mean would I take on a dizzy blonde with a potential opportunity for me, rather than a fellow, yes. Probably.' He laughed as he added 'Only joking. No, all would have to have the ability first'.

Finally Chris said 'I realise now why no-one talked to me about sexuality. My dad was 60 when he had me and my mum was 28. She had disseminated sclerosis. She died when I was 16. The disease works on the brain. She couldn't even feed herself, so there was no way she was going to tell me about the facts of life. I remember it started when we were out walking. She would just trip up over a paving slab, then she needed a walking stick, then a wheelchair and then she was confined to bed. That's why I was sent to boarding school at seven because she had to be hospitalised.' Chris spoke calmly and slowly but he was sad as he remembered about his childhood hurt and of his mother's life and death.

CASE STUDIES

Analysis

Chris, like so many other male managers, stated that as a boy sex wasn't talked about when he was small and also that masturbation was his first sexual experience.

However, he fell into the small percentage of men who had changed their attitude towards their early messages.

He demonstrated the importance and necessity of being able to manage personnel fairly and ensure that staff are fairly treated. More so, his links with his early memories of his mother were important for him.

I now give you my reasons for choosing the following case studies.

Nick

One (Nick) was chosen as an example of a male who had a Roman Catholic background and demonstrates how this affected his sexuality at work. (4, see Chapter 3). These revelations preceded the outcry in 1995 when several cases of priests abusing young children came to light. When Nick disclosed his sexual experiences with his priest to me in 1991 he considered his story to be highly unusual, as I did, little realising just how many children had been abused in similar ways, as has been documented now.

Vivienne

Another (Vivienne) demonstrates a change of attitude from 'Sex is wrong; it should be done privately' to 'It should be discussed; it should be open with no hang-ups. It should be enjoyed and funny; it can be fun.' She also demonstrates the analysis of one of the commonest stories told 'look how someone of high status behaved so badly'. Vivienne was also selected for 'sex role' affirmation as discussed in Chapter 3.

CASE STUDIES

Steve
The third subject (Steve) highlights the issues of confidentiality when two senior managers are having an affair, the 'Pillow Talk' syndrome. Steve demonstrates that early messages are still relevant now he is a senior manager. He admits that sexuality does affect him at work, both with students and staff.

Pru
Number Six (Pru) emphasises the difficulty for the subject to break out of her sex role (Chapter 3) and how she has finally achieved it. She also offers a story of achieving some feeling of self-worth.

Andy
Number nine (Andy) demonstrates the emotional feelings of anger and power and his need to work on his sexuality in ongoing directive counselling. He highlights the effect on him of having sex with students.

Fiona
Number eight (Fiona) gives a female perspective of the effect of Roman Catholicism on her. She has experienced cognitive dissonance and her sexuality was affected at work (attribution theory), and shadowing – by giving the qualities of her father to a male colleague at work.

Paul
The seventh case study gives a different perspective of homosexuality. As a gay male Paul is happy, has a full social life and he believes that his openness had actually gained him promotion, unlike so many other gays in the study who feared coming out.

CASE STUDIES

Hilary
The fourth was selected because of her traumatic childhood experiences and sexual orientation. She felt that she had overcome her early childhood sexual abuse. She demonstrated how difficult it is for her to be open about her preferred sexual practices as a lesbian.

Bryan
He was the fifth case study chosen, again for his different sexual preference from the majority, that is, for his bisexuality. Bryan displayed how his early memories to 'look for beauty in people' had been retained and how they affected him in interviews and relationships at work.

Chris
Lastly number ten (Chris) offers a perspective on the manager's role in terms of personnel management. He demonstrates how legislation can underpin a director's changing behaviour to ensure that profits are not wasted on paying out compensation fines.

All these case studies were sent to the participants, each of whom made alterations either to ensure confidentiality, or to clarify some part of the written case study. Nine out of the ten have either written to me or spoken to me, in person or by telephone since their interviews, updating me on their progress.

Where are they now?
The managers were interviewed between 1989 and 1997, so several years have passed since some of the interviews took place. What has happened to them since? (Some details have been omitted to maintain confidentiality.)

CASE STUDIES

Nick – Recognising his problem with touching, Nick maintains that he is much more comfortable with both men and women at work. He has been promoted at work. The media revelations in 1995 about the sexual abuse of children by priests and abuse in residential homes made him aware that his own experience was by no means unique.

Vivienne – Left the college and started up her own business. She has done very well financially but more importantly to her she now has job satisfaction! She no longer has to be involved with all the sexual subterfuge.

Steve – Left his job but stayed with his wife. Initially Steve and Mary saw each other regularly after he first left the college, but gradually the meetings stopped entirely, partly because of the distance between them. Now Steve's relationship with his wife is good and there is no social contact with his lover. 'We're (he and his wife) getting on much better now and I don't want any more of that heavy stuff with Mary.

Pru – Moved from the post in which I interviewed her and was then internally promoted within the new establishment. She did not marry Ted, but when he gained a new post she stayed with him in his new town house at weekends. They have now told some colleagues about their relationship. Pru tells me she now feels so much more confident about both her sexuality and her job. She says that she realises now just how powerful her messages were to her and she was glad that she had worked through them.

Andy – Now has retired from the prison service, set up in private practice and started an art group. He has private clients for counselling and contributes to educational training occasionally. There are still sexual difficulties with his wife, but he is now painting and finds that this gives him a real buzz.

CASE STUDIES

Fiona – I lost touch with Fiona about nine months after the interview (1993) but she sent a card to me a month after our meeting which read:

> *I've done it – talked with Howard! Life is much more harmonious. Now to tackle the rest of my ghosts! Lots of love and thank you.*

Paul – Is enjoying his work, enjoying his social life and still with his partner.

Hilary – Opened up a small business in a busy city centre with her partner. Although it is early days she thinks that it will do well. She and her partner still try to hide the fact that they are gay.

Bryan – Is living alone. His last relationship broke down but he sees his son regularly and has just found a new lover. As he said 'I'm in love again. It's wonderful at my age.'

Chris – Is still Managing Director of the national chain of shops. Enjoying his work and presently dealing with a case of harassment.

Summary

These ten case studies demonstrate the aspects of sexuality at work explored in Chapter 3. They give specific examples of how early sexual messages do affect managers as adults, how early religious instruction may continue to influence managers, show different homosexual and bisexual behaviour and attitudes [50, 51]. They also give examples of sexual harassment and incest, sexuality being used in interviews, of sexual jokes and innuendoes, of women's dress being seen as sexual, pillow talk, cognitive dissonance, conflict resolution and attitude change.

CASE STUDIES

Although the research began to look at how sexuality affected managers at work, what transpired was that many individual subjects were able to identify and resolve some of their childhood stoppers so that their 'crumple button' (pressed by negative feelings or thoughts) could change into a 'chuff button' (pressed by positive feelings or thoughts).

A further manifestation that emerged was the number of interviewees who talked about the deaths with which they had had to deal. Their grief had been buried alive instead of buried dead. So many people still carry their unresolved feelings about death around with them, even decades after the event. Crying helps but if you still believe that 'Big Boys Don't Cry' then these tears are suppressed. When we cry we are crying for ourself so the tears shown at funerals can be for our previous losses, not necessarily for the one being mourned at the time. This I believe was the case at Princess Diana's funeral. Many people felt they were given permission to grieve for their own losses.

CHAPTER 7

DISCUSSION AND CONCLUSIONS

What aspects of sexuality emerged from the research?

This work which was mainly with heterosexuals, but a few (5%) bisexuals and homosexuals, found that there were some gender differences in how sexuality affected managers at work, although it is important to recognise that this was not the intention of the research. 'The theory fits the data not the data fits the theory' [56].

Within the research findings there are some attitudes, behaviour and experiences that are shared by men and women, whilst other sexual messages, experiences and behaviour appear to affect only one gender. Here I summarise those aspects of the findings that are shared, then identify those experienced by women managers and then highlight those by male managers.

Men and women managers

Managers of both genders related how they were greatly affected by their sexuality at work, but experienced this in different ways. The stories told were about how being sexually involved with influential people contributed to their being promoted at work. In interviews, there was an uncertainty as to how to behave. Participants could be affected by their gender roles. Should they be aggressive or submissive? What was expected of them as a man or a woman? They were perhaps aware of sex typing when either being interviewed or interviewing, as in the case of giving more consideration to women with children.

In meetings managers' sexuality was experienced in terms of the following emotions: feelings of being excited, dismissed, second class, powerful, powerless, needing support, sexually uncomfortable or feeling more at ease with a particular gender. Individuals sometimes felt more at ease with colleagues of the same gender, and sometimes with the opposite. Affairs between staff were foremost in the sexual messages and sexual stories that were told about the organization. Sexual roles and gender issues were often highlighted by the managers.

It is also important to recognise that some managers perceived that their sexuality did not affect them at work at all (9%). However, as I worked through the interview with a few (five) from this group it became apparent to them that the reverse was the case. Nevertheless, some (11) maintained that they left their sexuality at home, a stance reminiscent of people who say that they leave their emotions at home.

In terms of childhood influences on sexuality there were shared experiences of religious teachings, leaving some of the managers with feelings that sex was wicked. For others, sex was enjoyable but there were conditions attached to this state usually linked with it being enjoyable in marriage. Others shared the influence that certain career implications could arise if they became pregnant or fathered a child either before their studies or apprenticeships were completed, and/or so sex could affect their job prospects. Careers could also be ruined if they married 'beneath' themselves. There were many 'don't' messages and certainly 'nice girls don't' ideas shared by both genders. Many of the difficulties that managers shared at work were linked by them to their early influential sexual stereotyping.

DISCUSSIONS AND CONCLUSIONS

Men and women managers experienced a change in attitude towards sexuality during their lives but my research demonstrates strongly how more women than men changed their early messages. Could this be because women are more likely to share their feelings with other women (or men) and as a result they are able to recognise their early messages? So in recognising the detrimental effect of negative sexual messages, maybe they decided to change them. Or maybe as women are the bearers of children, mothers are more likely to discuss their sexuality openly with other women, particularly during and after pregnancy. There is an intimacy at ante-natal clinics that men are unlikely to experience. Some men say that they share the intimacy of the rugby bath. I cannot verify this but from the stories that I am told the relationships would appear to be more like sexual horseplay rather than intimacy which is free of psychological game playing.

As well as the possibility of women more readily sharing their feelings, and sharing an intimacy with other women when pregnant, there is the experience of pregnancy itself which might affect sexual attitudes like 'docile pregnant ladies' [51]. Women are expected to divulge their sexual behaviour and exhibit their genitalia to medical strangers on a regular basis. In terms of cognitive dissonance, if a woman had been given 'sex is embarrassing' as an early message, then it is likely she would have to harmonise her thinking with the expected behaviour of sexual exposure in a medical setting. Another possible reason why more women than men change their sexual attitudes is the existence of women's groups where most women are able to share their feelings and offer mutual support. This may be different for men's groups, many of which revolve around sport, which in itself is competitive. Thus these groups may have a competitive framework where men are expected to play macho man rather than a supportive framework which enables men to share their feelings, although this may not be the case in men's groups like 'Children need Fathers'.

DISCUSSIONS AND CONCLUSIONS

If men shared their feelings more readily then possibly they would recognise their early messages and choose to change them. However, the very nature of some of the men's early messages may prevent them from discussing their feelings about sexuality. The model that emerges from this study is that the majority of the men in my sample had received messages of 'sex is not talked about' and 'Big Boys Don't Cry'. This implies that the latter is interpreted as 'men don't discuss feelings of grief or loss or don't get in touch with their internal sadness'. Even so, I find the statement that 'men don't show their emotions' to be nonsense. My experience is that men do show their emotions. Most do this in different ways to women — that is, they may more easily show emotions of anger, whilst women may be more comfortable with showing their feelings of grief. The flaw in all this maybe that I too am stereotyping too readily.

Another aspect which emerged from the research that might also add to sex stereotyping is that the majority of men, but only a small minority of women, experienced inner conflict about sexuality at work. So the argument that I offer is that if so many women are able to change their early sexual attitudes — hence experiencing less inner conflict about their sexuality at work — then maybe those men who do experience inner conflict could give some thought to one possible reason for this, which might be their retention of their early sexual messages.

Let us consider other reasons why men may experience inner conflict about their sexuality. Was it only because men do not change their attitude, or could there be other explanations? One explanation might be the question of role conflict and sex stereotyping, discussed more fully later, which may contribute to men's inner conflict. The age range of the men in the survey was 35 to 50 years. As the research took seven years to complete the age range went up pro-rata in 1996 to remove one of the variables of different managers in different generations. So many of the men may have been brought up with role models of women being the carers. Their mothers, whether working in employment or at home, may have given the men the model that women were there to look after men or to be submissive. Many women who were in employment in the past, were still the prime movers in looking after the house as well as being out all day at work. This may have been part of their mother's own role modelling when they were children.

Today many young men may not see women in this light, as equal opportunities have probably been part of their education. However, when some of the older male managers are faced with women taking senior posts to them or working as peers, then inner conflict between their expected female role model and the reality of what is happening at work may occur. If their mothers were employed it was likely that the majority of them still did everything in the home, maybe giving the impression that a career was secondary to their home commitments. Therefore some men may see female colleagues working only for pin money and so women are not taken seriously by all of the men.

A further issue for some men could be the legal aspects of their managerial role. They could be responsible for the health and safety of staff at work. There were incidents of men having an inner conflict when they had to tell a woman they were concerned about her being in an isolated working area late at night, without sounding sexist. Or they may have conflicts about the legal aspects of the Equal Opportunities Act whereby they are unable to specify a certain sex for a post but still feeling strongly that certain jobs mean certain sexes. Some of the men admitted to problems in appointing women for what they saw as men's jobs and vice-versa, again suggesting inner conflict with role models and sex stereotyping. They were also concerned about their own responsibility if things went wrong – what would happen if they sent a woman out on her own to do a job of work and she were to be attacked physically.

DISCUSSIONS AND CONCLUSIONS

Another reason for inner conflict – apart from men not changing their attitudes, role conflict or stereotyping – may be pure sexual attraction. Some men told me whether a woman is good or bad at her job it makes no difference to them in terms of how they treat her, meaning she would be treated in the same way as a man. If, however, the men felt sexually attracted to her then they would treat her differently, either being more dominant, nervous of her or not being able to work with her at all because of the sexual feelings involved. This phenomenon is encapsulated by one male manager saying:

My sexual feelings get in the way when working with a particular woman because I am physically erect in her presence at meetings, although she is the only woman who affects me in this way. I have a woman senior manager who I think is brilliant and many women colleagues – some great, some useless – but that is no different to the men I work with. It is only this particular woman. I spend a lot of my time trying to avoid her because I feel so turned on in her presence and that stops me from working effectively. I made excuses once for not going on a residential management training course with her because I was too scared of socialising with her. She may find me repulsive but I know if she gave me the slightest encouragement I would be unfaithful to my wife, which I never have been!

The existence of inner conflict in the majority of the men interviewed, is supported by the recognition of how so many of them justified their statements about sexuality, as seen in the research data (obtainable from the publisher).

Women managers

Now let us look at women managers. My findings showed that women managers were affected by their sexuality at work in interviews, where some of them addressed the issue of using their sexuality either to help them to attain promotion, new management posts, a different job role or to gain better grades at university. Others demonstrated how they had refused to use their sexuality to achieve promotion or be upgraded by tutors. Dressing in an appropriate manner was only an issue presented by the women and sometimes this took the form of dressing down their sexuality. Many women claimed that 'power' dressing was essential for them especially when they were the only woman in a senior management team, whilst many other women admitted to dressing in order to attract the opposite sex. Only a few women (3%) said that they dressed to attract the same sex. This is not to say that few women dress to gain approval or compete with other women. It is only what emerged from the interviews. A specific question had not been addressed.

The sexual messages and sexual stories of the organization encompassed the issue of equal opportunities which related to jobs, roles, power or powerlessness. The women were willing to admit to using their sexuality, and the organizational stories about female promotions due to sexual liaisons supported this notion.

Early sexual messages of the women, which differed from those of the men, were strongly related to the state of marriage. (No sex until you are married or sex only being acceptable in marriage.) Sex being something that women had to endure and experience of embarrassment were common themes. Many said that their first sexual experience (being full penetrative sex) happened when they were married. But in terms of the many meanings of sexuality, many women identified petting or orgasm as their first sexual experience rather than vaginal penetration, which many of the men seem to assume were women's first sexual experiences. Being raped or sexually abused left some of the women in states of sexual unease in the company of men. Yet again the issue of disclosure for the first time – or if not for the first time, recalling traumatic unfinished business – created the need for love, support and empathic counselling. Again, emphasising the need for researchers studying sexuality to be trained in counselling skills.

Male managers
The difference that emerged from the findings was that when the men talked about their sexuality they added justifications for their behaviour, especially when disclosing having affairs with, or being attracted to, people at work. Cases of having affairs with customers were only revealed by the men. There were a significant number of references made to sex typing and roles and admissions of uncertainty on how to relate or behave towards women at work. The element of projection was apparent with some of the men, as they rejected looking at their own emotions about sexuality and behaviour but were prepared to single out other staff at work who they thought were affected by their sexuality.

Chauvinistic behaviour from both sexes was part of the perceived sexual messages and stories at work that were identified by some of the men. 'Male chauvinism still abounds', 'female chauvinism exists', and 'beware of female guile' were what some (25%) were picking up as organizational messages. Having noted that some of the men did not want to explore their own feelings, by checking their early recalled childhood messages it was found these individuals had been offered either 'sex is not to be talked about' or 'Big Boys Don't Cry' messages which may have changed over the years into 'men don't disclose their emotions'.

Another category (50 or more made up a category) emerged from the men interviewed who were given early messages about homosexuality and these took the form of the abnormality. Macho imaging was inferred in many different ways. As with the summary about the women, the majority (80%) of the men did not change their early sexual attitudes and did identify many aspects of the conflicts that they experienced at work. One can only assume that if attitudes change then conflict may be reduced. However, one cannot know this for certain, but it is more likely. The case of discovering their sexuality in different ways and identifying masturbation as their first sexual experience was applicable only to the men. This is not to say that any of these identified differences are only applicable to one gender, but rather that these differences were identified by the particular men and women managers that I interviewed.

The effect of the research on me

As one becomes older and, hopefully wiser, new experiences become fewer. However, it was new for me to experience so many emotions at the same time during my research. Joy, frustration, love, anger, elation, depression, fear, insecurity, anguish, panic and the feeling of being valued were all mixed together for me throughout the seven years of my study. The feelings were not always in the same permutations but I cannot recall ever experiencing feeling totally confident about either what I was doing or why I was embarking on such a daunting project as sexuality. The last year was the exception, by which time I was more confident when I was interviewing more managers to enhance and validate the initial research findings

Why did I choose this subject? I think that there were three reasons: my past, present and future motives. Firstly, my past – having been professionally involved in how people were affected by their sexuality at work, but also professionally being seen (or thought to be seen) as working on soft options, people's feelings, not facts. But as stated in the introduction, I believe feelings are facts. Also there was the matter of my own past experience of my sexual messages being taboo and which were indeed linked to my mother, who died when I was seven. There was an aura of mystery around my mother given to me by my aunt, my mother's sister whom I adored, and reinforced by my cold unloving stepmother, of whom I tried for 40 years to please and to gain her approval. I did not succeed. She died cutting me out of her will, her final act of hate. I was told that my mother was bad, wicked and sexy and I must not be, otherwise I would end up like her. Maybe this also motivated me to finally grasp the nettle and research into the difficult area of childhood messages.

Secondly, my present work involves me in freelance management training that I choose and in more intimate, game-free relationships with management teams in varying organizations, and often I will hear their sexual stories. Another reason for undertaking this research may be that I wanted to understand more fully the sexual dynamics of other organizations. In addition, I think I wanted to make my subject credible. People skills are often scorned by many managers, staff and academics but I believe strongly in the value of such inter- and intra-personal skills.

Thirdly, I hope my findings will open doors for other researchers, but most of all that individuals might benefit from any worthwhile study that I produce: making links with their past, recognising the connections and working towards a more enriched life by discarding their negative psychological blocks about their sexuality.

I now look at how the research affected me in terms of the seven years taken to complete the study [56] emphasise the importance of having a framework before starting a study.

He (the researcher) must have a perspective that will help him see relevant data and abstract significant categories from his scrutiny of the data.

Thank goodness literature has moved on so that it now includes references to the female – his or her, he or she etc. – rather than using the male as a general example. When I started, I had an outer and an inner framework; the outer consisted of several questions that covered the areas I was keen to research (early recalled experiences, sexual stories of self and others at work) and the need to find material in order to achieve a rigorous study. Meanwhile, my inner framework was of a counselling role, the effect of such an encounter on the subject and my ethical responsibility. I explained my ethical stance to the individual interviewees. At the same time I wanted to give the subjects space and opportunity to tell their story uninterrupted, elaborating on the points that *they* felt were important. Hence the interviews were a mixture of the story they wanted to tell and the story I wanted to hear. So both the outer and inner frameworks dictated the structure before I started the study and the gathering of relevant data.

The semi-structured in-depth research interview technique was in contrast to many of my previous beliefs and practices. I was now going to be pointing people along my paths rather than those which they (the subjects) wanted to take. After a number of interviews I changed my approach and became less concerned with finding data but more able to let the subject go where they wanted to. This was all part of my own research development which I realised when discovering John Rowan and Peter Reason's work [52]. In particular, reference was made to Rowan's research cycle, initially used as a perspective on the 'standard alienated research project'. I found this a useful tool in trying to unravel the inner confusion that this research had created in me. (See Fig. 2.)

How this research cycle can be used by a researcher is explained by Rowan.

> *One is working in a particular field (BEING) and finds or is given a problem. One searches the literature to find if anyone has already tackled it, and mentally combines the information to refine the problem (THINKING). One then designs a research plan and discusses it with one's supervisor or colleagues (PROJECT). One then conducts an experiment, or carries out the survey or observations*

DISCUSSIONS AND CONCLUSIONS

(ENCOUNTER). One does one's data processing, content analysis, statistical manipulation, etc. (MAKING SENSE). And one writes the paper, or dissertation, or thesis (COMMUNICATION) and perhaps talks about it at conferences and other meetings, or writes an article about it, before returning to one's normal work in the field again (BEING).

I now demonstrate how the research affected me by using this cycle but I have adapted the language to suit my involvement. How I felt about the research was a predominant effect on me as a researcher. (See Fig. 3.).

Figure 2. Dialectical research cycle (after Rowan and Reason 1981)

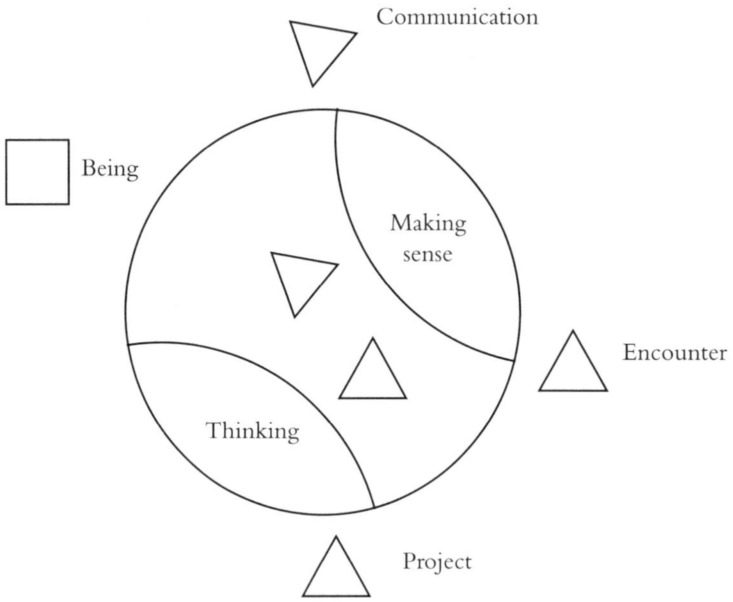

DISCUSSIONS AND CONCLUSIONS

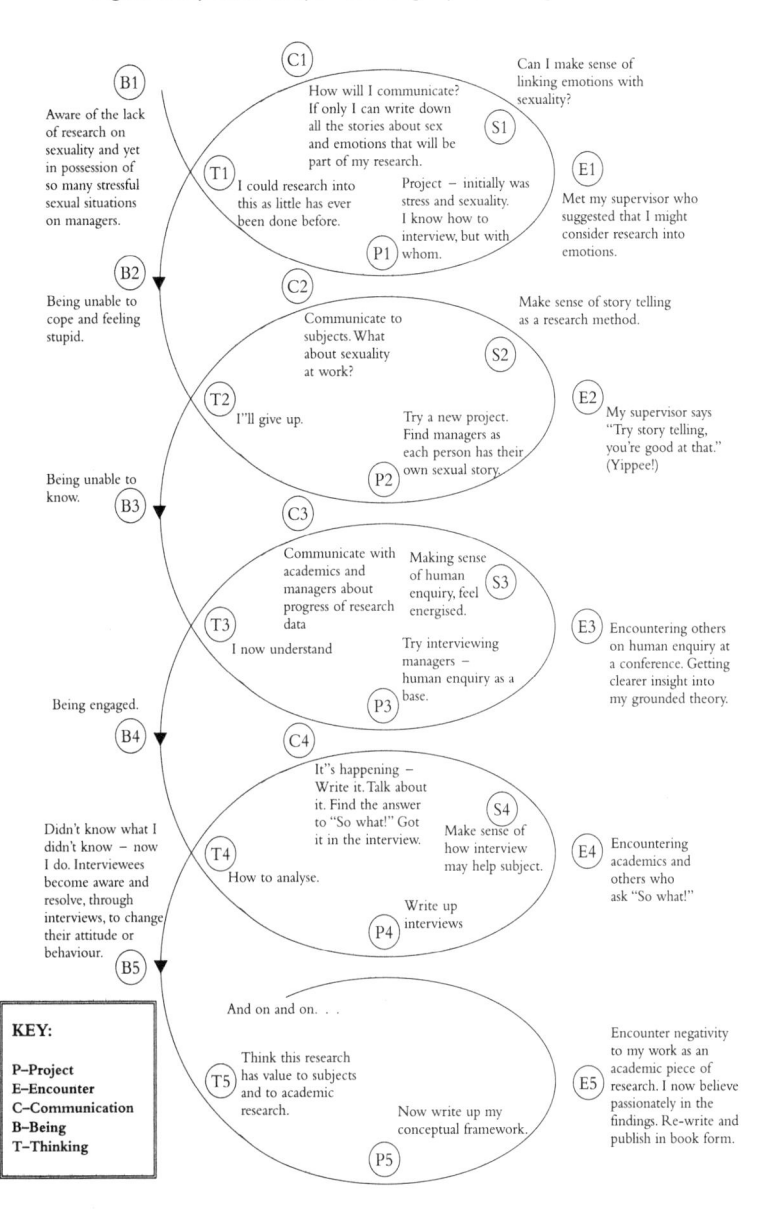

Figure 3. My research cycle showing my research process

- **B1** Aware of the lack of research on sexuality and yet in possession of so many stressful sexual situations on managers.
- **C1** How will I communicate? If only I can write down all the stories about sex and emotions that will be part of my research.
- **S1** Can I make sense of linking emotions with sexuality?
- **T1** I could research into this as little has ever been done before.
- **P1** Project – initially was stress and sexuality. I know how to interview, but with whom.
- **E1** Met my supervisor who suggested that I might consider research into emotions.

- **B2** Being unable to cope and feeling stupid.
- **C2** Communicate to subjects. What about sexuality at work?
- **S2** Make sense of story telling as a research method.
- **T2** I'll give up.
- **P2** Try a new project. Find managers as each person has their own sexual story.
- **E2** My supervisor says "Try story telling, you're good at that." (Yippee!)

- **B3** Being unable to know.
- **C3** Communicate with academics and managers about progress of research data
- **S3** Making sense of human enquiry, feel energised.
- **T3** I now understand
- **P3** Try interviewing managers – human enquiry as a base.
- **E3** Encountering others on human enquiry at a conference. Getting clearer insight into my grounded theory.

- **B4** Being engaged.
- **C4** It"s happening – Write it. Talk about it. Find the answer to "So what!" Got it in the interview.
- **S4** Make sense of how interview may help subject.
- **T4** How to analyse.
- **P4** Write up interviews
- **E4** Encountering academics and others who ask "So what!"

- **B5** Didn't know what I didn't know – now I do. Interviewees become aware and resolve, through interviews, to change their attitude or behaviour.
- And on and on. . .
- **T5** Think this research has value to subjects and to academic research.
- **P5** Now write up my conceptual framework.
- **E5** Encounter negativity to my work as an academic piece of research. I now believe passionately in the findings. Re-write and publish in book form.

KEY:
P–Project
E–Encounter
C–Communication
B–Being
T–Thinking

DISCUSSIONS AND CONCLUSIONS

A further specific effect on me has been an awareness of certain competencies and lack of others. Here I use the model of competence steps illustrated by O'Conner and Seymour [61] to demonstrate the different effects on me. (See Fig. 4.)

Figure 4. Model of competence steps

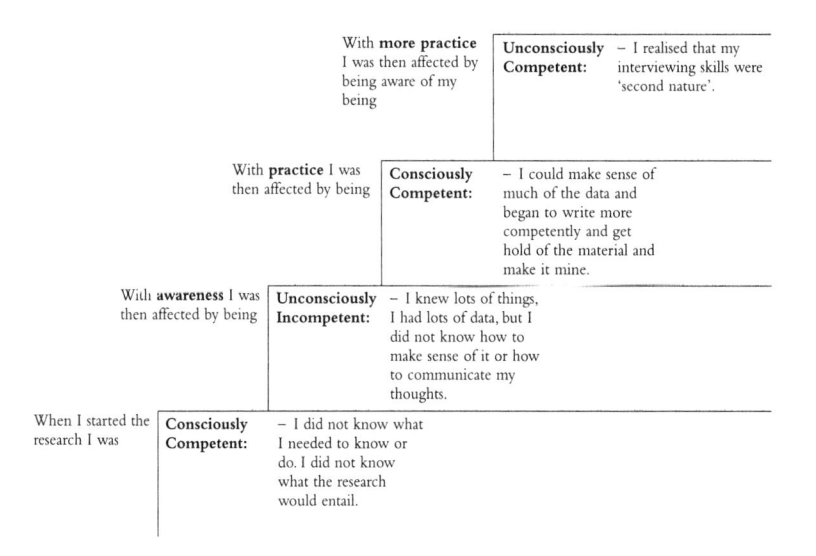

		With **more practice** I was then affected by being aware of my being	**Unconsciously Competent:** — I realised that my interviewing skills were 'second nature'.
	With **practice** I was then affected by being	**Consciously Competent:**	— I could make sense of much of the data and began to write more competently and get hold of the material and make it mine.
With **awareness** I was then affected by being	**Unconsciously Incompetent:**	— I knew lots of things, I had lots of data, but I did not know how to make sense of it or how to communicate my thoughts.	
When I started the research I was	**Consciously Competent:**	— I did not know what I needed to know or do. I did not know what the research would entail.	

As well as being affected by my past, present and future motives and range of different competencies, I was aware of the need to put people before the research, especially in the case of confidentiality.

Having stated that I needed an ethical framework in which to operate, I found that the issue of confidentiality was stressful and it was difficult for me when writing up my findings. Some managers were likely to be identified, perhaps by their ethnic origin, gender, title, status or demographic settings, therefore sections were omitted, names were changed. But there was still another difficulty. Those managers selected to be case studies may have told part of their sexual story to someone else, whereupon the rest of their story could be attributed to it, and the confidential nature of the work would be broken. As well as the strain of maintaining confidentiality there was also the emotional aspect of the work. In some of the interviews old scar tissues were broken, many tears were shed and feelings of anger were experienced as subjects recalled and made connections with what had happened to them sexually at home and at work. Sometimes there was a need for in-depth counselling as a separate process to the research interview.

There were times when I became so overpowered and overwhelmed by all the sexual stories about work that I wondered if anyone ever went to work, to work! The research also affected me in that for some of the time I felt sexually numb. So much anguish, so much unhappiness was being shared with me, that it seemed to stick to me. Only by writing up the data was I able to free myself from this feeling of being submerged in contaminated waters. Some stories I heard shocked me, although I hope I did not show it. I do not wish to be specific because of hurting the people involved, but I was upset by the amount of pain that child abuse had caused people.

Initially one of my main motives for this research was to try to bridge the gap between extremist views of 'all men are' or 'all women are'. I set out thinking that I might be able to show the similarities of both genders, maybe that of wanting to be loved and valued and to give the other sex's point of view. I did not want to look at gender solely, as such studies tend to focus on the differences, rather than on the similarities. So, another effect of the research on me was that I was surprised by some of the findings that emerged in the different categories of men and women managers, particularly the gender difference in attitude change. Even so, there were some shared feelings and behaviour that might help people to see that they are not alone, that both men and women managers do share some aspects of how their sexuality affects them at work. Although I have written about the stressful effects on me, there were also many interviews that were great fun, with lots of laughter which may have been used as a nervous release of tension.

When I began the research I was unaware of how much ground I would have to cover. The work was not a problem but the psychological effect was painful. Having completed the research, the major effect on me now is that although it was difficult, intensive, emotive and stressful because it became the most important thing in my life and contaminated my personal and social life, it was very worthwhile, rewarding and personally enriching.

The practical significance of this research

Within the corporate world of managers and their staff there are many group dynamics, some of which go unnoticed by the majority of people in those organizations. We have come a long way in the last two decades with the implementation of equal opportunity policies but creating legal frameworks does not necessarily remove the emotional and attitudinal aspects of how we feel about the opposite or the same sex. These concepts are deeply rooted in the psyche and this research offers just one way of observing how or if managers are affected by their sexuality at work. Looking at early sexual messages, as described in the literature review, offers one way to research this phenomenon and this has its limitations, so I chose to look at sexual stories as well. Studying in-depth childhood experiences, rather than scratching the surface of a number of other theories, e.g. learning theory, nature/nurture arguments, or solely considering gender issues at work, was found to be an effective strategy. So this research may be relevant to the academic community, to managers, the therapeutic community, to educators/management trainers, and to the management literature.

DISCUSSIONS AND CONCLUSIONS

Relevance to the academic community

I believe that this research is of particular significance to the academic research community as it attempts to look at a daunting subject that is so lacking in research on management issues – sexuality in organizations. It may be of interest to those academics who find the area of early recalled childhood messages and their effect on the behaviour of adults as fascinating as I do. After searching through literature thoroughly no other research of this nature was found. Therefore this research could influence the literature on management and organizations to which academics refer. Also it may illuminate some of the hidden aspects of organizational life. This study may inspire academics or postgraduate research students to explore other aspects of sexuality in organizations and it could open doors for further research by people interested in the area of personal growth. Other students may wish to pursue the research on early recalled messages – perhaps on religion, education, money, marriage, gender or success – and endeavour to find out if these are still carried and how (or if) they affect managers at work. The possibilities are endless.

Relevance to managers

This study could be important to the world of managers, their literature, training, performance and self-awareness. It may improve managerial effectiveness when dealing with issues of gender, equal opportunities, sexual harassment, making meetings effective (understanding the effects of sexuality in both formal and informal meetings). Relationships may be improved when people realise the underlying sexual forces that are around when they are carrying out their everyday tasks. Interviewing skills may improve due to the new knowledge, when individuals are undergoing interviews for appraisal, staff development, new roles, performance-related pay, appointments, disciplinary purposes, dealing with conflict or promotion. Managers themselves may become more aware of the issues of sexuality that are present in the group dynamics of their staff and may be able to discuss these situations more openly rather than turn a blind eye. They may become more comfortable with their own sexuality or be able to analyse more effectively the dynamics of what is happening between themselves and their staff. Perhaps they will be able to come to terms with one of the reasons why they relate more comfortably with some staff and not with others.

Relevance to the therapeutic community

Many therapists, psychoanalysts, counsellors, medics, social workers and others are familiar with the concept of early childhood experiences possibly affecting adult sexuality. They may use this research as part of their work, counselling sessions or training. To date there has been little academic research on the effect of early sexual messages, but some work has been done on alcoholics by Claude [53] in his book 'Games Alcoholics Play'. This was considered to be one of the most worthwhile pieces of research ever carried out in the helping of alcoholics.

A further piece of research on early messages was carried out by Robin Norwood [54] in her book *Women Who Love Too Much*. (This theme could also apply to men who love too much.) She found that women continued with their early messages throughout adult life in terms of finding a mate. She advised that women needed to break with or change their early negative messages, firstly recognising them and then changing them, in order to make progress in improving their life and intimate relationships.

Another book, *Families and How to Survive Them* by Robin Skinner and John Cleese [21], also offers people the opportunity of recognising early messages and how to break free of them. Unfortunately these works are considered pop psychology and denigrated by many in the academic community which is a shame because they have probably helped a lot of people.

DISCUSSIONS AND CONCLUSIONS

Relevance to educators and management trainers

This research may be of interest to educators and trainers and gives some insight into the issues of sexuality when teaching, and when attempting to create an enabling learning environment. Educators may be skilled enough to draw their members' attention to the sexuality that is ever present in a group. Attention may be given to the sexual elements of management training when courses and or seminars are planned. It may be that the issue of managing sexuality is included in the many management training courses, most of which today are in-service training but others include the Master of Business Administration (MBA) courses and The Management Charter Initiative (MCI) programmes. The latter involves managers having their competence assessed at work, all very subjective areas where sexuality will certainly be present. To date no university or college syllabuses on management training includes any aspect of dealing with sexuality at work. I feel that this is a disgrace.

Relevance to management literature

As I explained earlier, there is a dearth of knowledge about sexuality in management literature. My research may be relevant to future writers on the subject of management and could give permission for sexuality to be part of the everyday helpful management literature.

Staff do not leave their sexuality and emotions at home when they come to work. They bring it with them. Managing sexuality is just as necessary a skill for managers as is dealing with the paperwork!

Conclusion

Undoubtedly sexuality does affect managers at work. This statement emerges from my research. Here I develop how they are affected and offer a list of observations for managers. Then I consider the flaws in the study. The ways managers are affected can be seen in four ways, by their:

DISCUSSIONS AND CONCLUSIONS

1). sexual attitudes
2). sexual stereotyping
3). behaviour towards the opposite or same sex
4). reaction to the organizational sexual messages and stories at work

I argue here that early childhood sexual messages and sexual experiences can contribute to the formation of sexual attitudes – which in themselves may affect sexual stereotyping, sexual behaviour and certain reactions to organizational messages and stories. This belief is based on my literary search, experience and research.

The formation of certain sexual attitudes may be in contradiction to expected managerial performance e.g. a manager that is told as a child that 'sex is only between men and women' and then in adulthood has to make a decision to allocate accommodation for a 'gay group' may be affected by his or her sexual attitude. Or the manager who had received a message of 'sex should not be talked about' may find that discussing an HIV policy makes them feel uncomfortable. Or the manager who has had religious messages that abortion is a sin may have difficulty if involved in a medical or welfare support service that wishes to develop an open service for contraception, or establish medical links for abortion. Or if they are told or it is inferred that girls stay at home and look after their children then the manager is likely to find it difficult to support requests for crèches or find backing for such ventures.

Just as managers' attitudes may be affected by their sexual messages, so these attitudes may also affect sexual stereotyping. That is, 'boys do this, girls do that,' in terms of allocating suitable areas of work to staff. Perhaps you believe that there are certain things men can do and women can't and vice versa. Inner conflict may result from early attitudes that influence sex stereotyping, e.g. women's roles for caring supportive jobs, men's roles for powerful controlling jobs. So these early messages may also act as a filter in the perception of sex roles, which may lead to cognitive dissonance, a lack of inner harmony. Their early messages are at odds with their expected behaviour e.g. early message: 'Men have to work and look after women, so they can bring up the children,' but your present expected behaviour is to 'do what your female boss tells you'. These views just don't connect, so inner conflict can arise.

Gender stereotyping is displayed in the behaviour of some managers where in meetings women may find themselves marginalised by men or men may find themselves excited by the presence of particular women or men. Their behaviour may be that of avoiding eye contact or uncomfortable body language.

Sexuality may also affect managers in the way in which they behave at interviews or in appraisals; making allowances for women with children or not appointing an interviewee because of being sexually attracted to them or gaining or losing promotion because of a sexual liaison with some person in authority.

Furthermore in terms of stereotyping and behaviour, the language used may also be indicative of sexuality at work. For instance, a male manager may say 'well done' to a female colleague. She may respond with 'You're only saying that because I'm professional' but when the same manager criticises her the response may be 'You're only saying that because I'm a woman!' Thus this demonstrates the difficulty that some men have experienced. This could apply equally to some male staff. Women may also indicate by their language that they give sexual power to men – 'I work for him' or 'He is my boss'. The spoken interactions can also be symptomatic of sexual behaviour between men and men, for instance, horseplay or power games.

How managers react to the sexual messages and organizational sexual stories is also a facet of how sexuality affects managers at work. Some staff may leave, or be asked to leave. This may be because they have brought the difficulties stemming from certain sexual behaviour to the attention of senior management. However, because managers are more likely to turn a blind eye [35] then it is more likely that the reason for leaving would be because some staff are unable to handle working with people with whom they have had an affair (feelings that sex is wrong which may lead to guilt); feel usurped or undermined by new sexual relationships that have emerged (conflict or there may be envy); feel threatened or insecure by having to work with certain colleagues because of their gender or sexual attractiveness or harassment; (stereotyping which may also involve fear); think they are being discussed or discriminated against, or feel humiliated because of their sexual liaisons; recognise their promotion prospects have stopped due to a sexual relationship at senior management level that blocks their progress or feel that confidentiality is impossible because of the 'pillow talk' [12] that abounds in their organization.

So what? If senior managers believe that they are effective as well as efficient then they may need to be aware of the sexual phenomena that exists at work. They may need to appreciate the sexual difficulties that may be being experienced in different ways by their male and female colleagues. To be able to recognise the signs is one thing but how to manage sexuality at work requires managers to develop more people skills. As more women become senior managers sexuality at work is likely to be more prevalent, not because women are more sexual but because there will be a change in the power base so women will have power over men.

CHAPTER 8

SO WHAT? HOW DOES THIS AFFECT ME AS A MANAGER?

The idea that sexuality affects managers at work is not new. The days of turning a blind eye to what is going on are long gone. Organizations in the UK have been taking sexual harassment more seriously over the last few years and some have devised policies for dealing with it, whilst in America organizations have been preoccupied with such cases for the last decade. Sexual relationships and how sexuality affects managers remains largely an issue for individual discretion. Can we risk leaving this complex area to common sense or outmoded rules any longer? Hence this chapter focuses on suggestions on how managers might be able to raise their awareness of this important aspect of management, and as a result manage more effectively.

SO WHAT? HOW DOES THIS AFFECT ME AS A MANAGER?

Having read the research we have already discussed, are you now considering what this might mean for you as a manager? Or how you are managed by your line manager or your relationships with colleagues at work?

I expect that by now you are more consciously aware of your own early childhood messages about sexuality and whether your attitude has changed. Or maybe you recognise that you are still carrying some of those thoughts or behaviour patterns. Perhaps you are still embarrassed by situations of a sexual nature or still believe sex is something not to be talked about. In which case you will need to learn to talk about it and become more comfortable with this important component of management. So this chapter covers and discusses what kind of role model you are as a manager; then looks at your sexuality; the sexuality of others; addresses sexuality at work; sexual harassment; and what can happen if you ignore sexuality at work — the consequences can be dire.

As demonstrated earlier, because sexuality is generally perceived as being private and personal it is probably one of the most difficult areas within your work force to address, so let us begin by looking at how comfortable you are with you sexuality and what kind of role model you provide? First, complete the following questionnaire:

Questionnaire 1: What kind of role model are you as a manager?

	Yes	No
1. Do any of your staff think that you are sexually involved with someone?	❏	❏
2. Does your behaviour suggest that you have favourites?	❏	❏

SO WHAT? HOW DOES THIS AFFECT ME AS A MANAGER?

		Yes	No
3.	Do you spend more time with some staff than others because you are sexually attracted to them?	❑	❑
4.	Have you been promoted because of some sexual liaison with a person of influence?	❑	❑
5.	Have staff commented to you about other people's sexual relationships or behaviour expecting you to address the difficulty but you have ignored their request?	❑	❑
6.	Have you witnessed sexual behaviour that seems inappropriate for the workplace but have refrained from commenting on it?	❑	❑
7.	Are you aware of any member of staff having difficulty in working with their line manager because he or she (the line manager) is sexually involved with another colleague but ignored dealing with it?	❑	❑
8.	Are you experiencing your lines of communication being blocked because of someone's sexual involvement with another colleague but not addressed the situation?	❑	❑
9.	Have you avoided speaking to individuals directly about how their sexuality is affecting other colleagues?	❑	❑
10.	Do your staff mistrust you to be able to handle and address situations of a sexual nature?	❑	❑

SO WHAT? HOW DOES THIS AFFECT ME AS A MANAGER?

How did you score? More than 3 'Yes' answers and you are a poor role model of a manager. Your staff are likely to be affected negatively by your management style.

Now let us consider your sexuality. As a manager have you ever found yourself experiencing any of the following situations? See Questionnaire 2. Have you been aware of the sexuality of others and wished that you were able to manage those situations more effectively? See Questionnaire 3.

Some of these points were raised in the introduction. Have your answers changed?

Questionnaire 2: Your sexuality

Have you ever:

		Yes	No
1.	preferred to be at work rather than at home because you are **sexually involved** with someone? (Sexually involved would be sexually intimate or hoping to be.)	❏	❏
2.	**promoted** people to whom you are sexually attracted?	❏	❏
3.	**promoted** anyone with whom you have had or are having a sexual relationship?	❏	❏
4.	**demoted** anyone to whom you are sexually attracted?	❏	❏
5.	**demoted** anyone with whom you have had or are having a sexual relationship?	❏	❏

SO WHAT? HOW DOES THIS AFFECT ME AS A MANAGER?

		Yes	No
6.	had an affair with a colleague or client? (An affair would be termed as a sexual relationship you may or may not wish other colleagues or partners to know about.)	❏	❏
7.	found that if you had an affair it negatively affected the way in which you worked?	❏	❏
8.	had time off work because of the effect of a sexual relationship?	❏	❏
9.	**appointed** someone to whom you are sexually attracted?	❏	❏
10.	deliberately **not appointed** someone to whom you were attracted for whatever reason?	❏	❏

More than three 'Yes' answers? Your sexuality is likely to be influencing you at work and your staff may be adversely affected by your behaviour.

This research offers two possible reasons for the situations outlined above: either managers worried about the possibility of starting a relationship, especially as a present partnership is difficult, or they are anxious about being able to work with someone who sexually arouses them.

Now think about the people with whom you work.

SO WHAT? HOW DOES THIS AFFECT ME AS A MANAGER?

Questionnaire 3: Sexuality of others

                                                                                                 Yes No

Would you be able to:

1. manage staff involved in a sexual relationship if you received a complaint? ❏ ❏

2. challenge someone about sexual innuendoes? ❏ ❏

3. address complaints of sexual harassment? ❏ ❏

4. handle the conflict between staff if a sexual relationship was involved? ❏ ❏

5. deal with an emotional male or female who wishes to discuss their personal concerns about an affair which has ended? ❏ ❏

6. work comfortably with someone of a different sexual orientation from yourself? ❏ ❏

7. set up support systems for people who are HIV positive? ❏ ❏

8. initiate and complete a policy for dealing with sexual relationships at work? ❏ ❏

9. support a pregnant, unmarried, member of staff who claims that another, married member of your staff is the father of the unborn child? ❏ ❏

SO WHAT? HOW DOES THIS AFFECT ME AS A MANAGER?

                                                                                                              Yes No

10. discuss with your senior manager his or her sexual behaviour which you think is affecting the workings of the organization?   ❏ ❏

More than three 'No' answers? Then you may have demotivated or angry staff who feel badly managed.

The author would be pleased to receive completed questionnaires. Please send them to Jean Civil, Meadway Farm, Westbury-sub-Mendip, Somerset, BA5 1HE.

Sexual harassment

Times are changing and with those changes you as a manager may also need to change your style of management. The changes may include women taking more senior managerial roles, a more predominant multi-cultural workforce, more women appointed in what has been regarded as 'men's jobs', the employment of staff with physical disabilities or special learning requirements, the cutting back of older staff at a younger age, or the financial requirements that can mean unemployment for some staff.

All of these situations can lead to different kinds of harassment. All the 'isms' can involve harassment – racial, disability, financial, gender, age and sexual harassment.

As a manager you will need to ensure that you are just as skilled at dealing with sexual harassment as you are with reorganising your workforce for better productivity, for the implications of ignoring such things is likely to affect your staff in the following ways:

1. Work productivity is likely to decrease.
2. Staff are unhappy if being harassed.

SO WHAT? HOW DOES THIS AFFECT ME AS A MANAGER?

3. Lack of management intervention worsens the situation.
4. Ongoing harassment demotivates people, innovation and energy levels are lowered.
5. Time is wasted avoiding the harasser.
6. Work time is spent talking about the situation.
7. Relationships are jeopardised permanently.
8. If trust is once broken it cannot ever be regained to the same extent.
9. Work becomes a joyless place to be.
10. Ultimately harassed staff may leave or take legal action against you as a manager or employer.

Sexual harassment is not always overt and many harassers are not necessarily aware of the effects of their behaviour. They can be acting through ignorance rather than malice.

Let us look at some of the definitions of sexual harassment.

A particularly degrading and unacceptable form of treatment which it must be taken to be the intention of Parliament to restrain'
(Strathclyde Regional Council v Porcelli)

'Unwanted conduct of a sexual nature or other conduct based on sex affecting the dignity of men and women at work. This can include unwelcome physical, verbal and non-verbal conduct'.
(EC Code of Conduct)

The EC code
Harassment is unacceptable if:

1. unwanted, unreasonable and offensive to the recipient
2. used as a basis for employment decisions (e.g promotion)
3. it creates intimidating, hostile or humiliating work environment

SO WHAT? HOW DOES THIS AFFECT ME AS A MANAGER?

Sexual harassment can be in the form of pestering, annoying, upsetting or wearing someone out with unwanted comments. Language is so important and many people can object to being called 'boy' or 'girl' whilst others may take offence about comments on their physical appearance even when they are supposedly meant in fun. You have to be so careful as a manager.

At the other end of the spectrum harassment can be physical abuse. Other possibilities could include blackmail and rumour mongering which has caused great distress to some people, even leading to suicide.

In America sexual harassment has been well documented – both cases and procedures. However, many managers are so concerned about doing the right thing that sometimes they go too far. Look at the following example.

Office rules for the American man
Sidney Siller, a New York lawyer and founder of The National Organization for Men, which claims to be the largest men's rights group in the US, has drawn up a list of 'Gentlemen's Rules for Survival in the Workplace' – some eminently sensible, others verging on the absurd – which he suggests should be followed in the workplace:

- Keep your office door open when a female co-worker visits your office. Invite your secretary or a colleague to be present.
- Do not ask a female colleague for a date. Do not mix work and courtship.
- If you are game enough to ask her out and she turns you down, do not ask again!
- Do not give her a lift or let her ride in your car when you are alone with her.

SO WHAT? HOW DOES THIS AFFECT ME AS A MANAGER?

- If a female co-worker makes a pass at you, give her the brush off.
- Do not tell any jokes that are lewd or suggestive.
- Do not proposition any co-worker.
- Do not have lunch, dinner or cocktails with female co-workers.
- Be precise in the manner in which you speak to a female co-worker.
- Do not make comments about a female co-worker's appearance. Do not tell her that she looks great or compliment her about the perfume or fragrance she wears.
- Do not put your arm around, massage, touch or embrace her.
- Do not discuss feminism, sex, abortion or erotic works of art.
- Do not use foul language in her presence.
- Do not be an office jerk, who winks or smirks at her. Do not flirt.
- Be prudent in your behaviour at office Christmas parties, retirement and farewell gatherings.
- Do not use any form of bribery in return for sexual favours.
- Do not humiliate or denigrate her work. Criticise constructively while rating her job skills.
- Do not ask a female co-worker about her personal life. In short DO NOT GET INVOLVED!
- Last but not least if a female co-worker appears to be suffering from PMT, do not ask if she's having a period.
- Remember! A false complaint of sexual harassment could ruin your career, your family and your life!

I now offer you:

10 managers' rules to prevent sexual harassment for men and women

1. Do not turn a blind eye when you have observed inappropriate sexual behaviour.

SO WHAT? HOW DOES THIS AFFECT ME AS A MANAGER?

2. Do not tell jokes that maybe construed as sexist or offensive.
3. Do not collude with sexual stories and rumours about staff – address them.
4. Do not refer to a person's anatomy.
5. Do not promote anyone with whom you are or were sexually intimate.
6. Do not use language that could offend male or female colleagues.
7. Do not make homophobic comments.
8. Do not touch or embrace staff without their permission.
9. Do not promise promotion or job changes in exchange for sexual favours.
10. Do not allow posters, calendars etc., of an erotic sexual nature to be displayed.

So as a manager you may also have to deal with allegations of sexual harassment. In these cases you need to be able to deal sensitively with both the accuser and accused. If you do not have a policy you will need to initiate one. Below is a checklist for you to consider in terms of understanding and empathising with the person experiencing the harassment. Also there is a list of suggestions of what you, as a manager may need to do.

The person experiencing harassment needs to:

1. Tell the person that they object to their behaviour or comments.
2. Act as quickly as possible when harassment occurs.
3. Write down what happened as soon as possible after the event.
4. Be able to say directly how he or she feels and describe the offensive behaviour.

5. Be prepared to tell his/her story in front of the harasser.
6. Seek confidential counselling from a trained counsellor.
7. Ask for emotional support.
8. Ask for help in writing the report.
9. Feel able to come into work knowing that he or she is safe from gossip and ridicule.
10. Choose an empathic senior manager who can be trusted to maintain confidentiality.

Managers need to:

1. Be aware that sexuality exists at work.
2. Inform all staff that sexual harassment will not be tolerated in the organization.
3. Remove offensive posters, calendars etc., displayed in work areas.
4. Address any comments or behaviour that may be construed as sexual harassment.
5. Talk directly to staff about their behaviour if there is a complaint.
6. Initially resolve the problem informally but if needed refer to a trained counsellor.
7. Treat what is disclosed to them in confidence and ask for a written report of the incidents, if the harassed person is willing.
8. Reassure the harassed person that their future prospects will not be affected by the incident or the allegations (and carry this out).
9. Implement a preventive policy for sexual harassment.
10. Know and understand disciplinary procedures.

SO WHAT? HOW DOES THIS AFFECT ME AS A MANAGER?

Recognise that your sexuality is likely to affect you and your colleagues at work, both positively and negatively. Positively, because sex can be fun, can motivate, excite, relieve stress, enlighten and enhance the workload. Negatively, because it can lead to sexual harassment, jealousy, rejection, betrayal, loss of trust, or job loss.

HEALTH WARNING

Refer staff to a trained counsellor if someone needs help. This is a specialised skill which requires training; do not try to do it yourself. I now offer you a list of tips.

Managing your own sexuality at work

In order to handle your sexuality at work you may wish to consider the following practices and suggestions.

Memories mould motives

Be aware that early sexual messages can influence the way that you and your staff may feel, believe and behave.

The fact that the greater percentage of men tend to continue with their early sexual messages would indicate that as a manager you may think about asking some of your staff what their early messages were and if they continue to carry such thoughts. Do not be surprised if some of them say 'sex was never discussed as a child' but now 'I talk about sex very easily'. It could be that they will jest but not necessarily feel comfortable discussing issues that differ from gender roles they have been brought up with; or they may be averse to the appointment of gay candidates; or for either sex to find it difficult working with a woman as their line manager. Take note of statements made to you in private about their real beliefs and values in such matters.

SO WHAT? HOW DOES THIS AFFECT ME AS A MANAGER?

Permanent prejudices

Take account of the way in which your early messages (maybe even those about race, religion, sexual orientation or gender) have left you with in-built prejudices and stereotyping.

These may affect you in discussion on sexual issues such as forming policies on HIV, establishing medical services for contraception or abortion referrals, initiating or finding accommodation for gay groups, crèches or taking affirmative action when making appointments to positions of power so that women, all races, disabled people or those of a different sexual orientation to yourself are represented.

Courting conflict

Realise that your early sexual messages can be changed, but if they cannot, remind yourself that, as a *male* manager, it is possible that you may be experiencing inner conflict about your sexuality.

As a *female* manager, remember that many male colleagues maybe undergoing inner conflict, with you as a woman line manager. This could also be the case for many of your staff for whom you have managerial responsibilities. Perhaps you can think of someone you know who may be struggling with their job role because of the person with whom they have to work.

Meetings can marginalise

Try to analyse the sexual dynamics in meetings. If you are a lone woman or man surrounded by colleagues all of the same sex, then you may feel isolated or marginalised. On the other hand, you may enjoy the scenario. If so, ask yourself why.

Some women or men may prefer to be the only representatives of their sex in a management team. It gives them that extra knowledge about their gender. Some women may even enjoy 'the Thatcher position' as a woman but actually work at preventing other women from joining them, rather than encouraging female promotions. Statements like 'I am the only woman on the executive' can be heard as 'I made it; other women can't.' It is a proud comment rather than a sad one.

Lovers liaisons break loyalty
Acknowledge that staff may feel negative towards the issue of confidentiality if you or other managers indulge in 'pillow talk' or have a sexual liaison with their colleagues. This can certainly lead to conflict.

Imagine that you have a line manager who is sexually involved with someone for whom you have a line management responsibility. You are dissatisfied with that member of staff's work. You want to discuss it with your line manager but you can't because you know that he or she will have discussed your managerial incompetence or mistakes with their lover (your line manager). It does not make for an easy life and can create a lot of problems. Sometimes you may be circumvented and decisions arrived at between the two of them in private may not be what you would wish. Cases have been illustrated where staff only have access to the director through their mistress, wife, lover or husband. This certainly creates annoyance, frustration even anger amongst staff. If couples are openly causing a problem then you as a manager have to establish a management structure that splits up such couplings so that other staff are able to work effectively and not be blocked by such strong pairs.

You also need to organize your organization.

Sexual stories Sensitise yourself to your organization's sexual messages and stories and ask yourself if you may be contributing towards them. What sexual messages do you emit?

Are you demonstrating a liaison with someone? Are you talked about because of your present or past sexual involvements with colleagues? Maybe you have confided in another member of staff about your liaison and that confidence has been broken, so now rumours have whizzed around the workplace. Maybe the relationship has broken down and the aggrieved partner has had their say about your shortcomings. If you hear stories about other people do not add to the rumours. If you are going to say anything then speak to the people concerned.

Preventive policies Introduce policies that are clear and concise and acceptable to staff, that declare openly the reasons for separating staff into different working areas or roles, especially in cases where particular liaisons are affecting others.

If you are told by someone that they are having problems because of a particular liaison then you need to address the situation. Only talk to them about what you have observed, not what other people have said to you. Say 'What I have observed is that you and. . . are now seen as an item and this appears to be causing problems as two of the staff do not appear to be working effectively in your team. It seems to me that they no longer have direct access to you as their line manager. That makes me feel concerned because previously you all operated well together. What I need is for you to resolve this situation by talking to the members of your team and establishing some ground rules.' Ask your staff if there are any issues that they want to discuss with you, in the presence of your partner.

If you say what you have *observed* rather than what you have been told, you will be listened to. People feel threatened if they think other staff have been telling you tales. If you say what you *feel*, people cannot argue with how you feel, they can argue with how you think but they cannot say 'you don't feel that'. Be clear in your own mind what you *need* from your staff. Prepare what you are going to say, don't just waffle, but say it directly.

SO WHAT? HOW DOES THIS AFFECT ME AS A MANAGER?

Handling harassment Deal with issues of sexual harassment, at first in a confidential way, and be sure of your facts and procedures. Avoid projecting your values and belief systems on to others.

Try to remain as objective as possible as sexual harassment often involves an imbalance of power. That is to say that usually it is the harasser who has the power which means that the harassed can have great difficulty making a complaint. You may think that sexual harassment is about lust for another person but harassment is more likely to be about wanting power over someone, and in fact means a dislike rather than a fondness for that individual.

Potent power Think about power issues, how some managers in your organization use their sexual or gender power over others (for instance, if one gender is under-represented).

Some people are also sexually excited by power and some of your staff or customers may be investing power in you. As a manager you will need to be able to distinguish when you are being propositioned because of your position and influence. Some staff may see you as a step on the promotion ladder if they endear themselves to you at whatever level of intimacy, regardless of your gender or sexual orientation. Also be aware of staff who may either threaten to accuse you of harassment because of your position, or, regardless of your position, genuinely feel that you are harassing them. So you need to guard yourself against such accusations. Therefore it is important that you use inoffensive language and relate openly and genuinely to your staff as against a sarcastic, sniggering, or slimy manner. Other power issues may stem from in the fact that you have the power or influence to appoint your lovers to positions of power. Be warned, this will really cause problems.

SO WHAT? HOW DOES THIS AFFECT ME AS A MANAGER?

Different desire drives Empathise with staff who are of a different sexual orientation to yourself.

Within your organization you will be working with people who do not share your particular sexual orientation, just as you will be working with people of a different race, culture, religion, gender – all of which needs to be recognised. Prejudice is built on fear and ignorance. So you will need to manage your own fears and ignorance. Try to see the world through others' eyes, listen through their ears, walk in their shoes. Sly comments can hurt even the most outwardly successful manager or employee. If you are heterosexual then remember that many homosexuals are scared of revealing their gay orientation for fear of the prejudice that they may have to endure at work. If you are homosexual then try to remember that heterosexuals may only see the world as having one type of sexual viewpoint so can often make natural assumptions in their speech and behaviour. This would also apply to the hurt that can be caused by assuming people have partners or families. People's stories are different but their hurt feelings are the same.

Right roles Recall that your perceptions of sex roles and sex stereotyping may not be shared by others and that different generations may have different attitudes.

Issues may depend upon your age. Maybe there is a generation gap between yourself and some of your colleagues reflected in sexual stereotyping. Forgetting political correctness for the moment, say out loud (unless you are reading this with others present) what you honestly think the role of a man should be. Is what you have said very different from what you would say at a management meeting? Now try the same thing with what you truly think the role of a woman should be! Again, are there any contradictions between what you say at work and what you inwardly feel? Certain generations

SO WHAT? HOW DOES THIS AFFECT ME AS A MANAGER?

grow up with different male and female role models so there are many older managers who still find it difficult to accept the changing role of men and women as we move to the next millennium. However, some men and women are still chauvinistic about their gender regardless of age, and find it difficult to work with the opposite sex in any kind of respectful or genuine way. To work in this negative environment can only bring you misery either in a joyless relationship or organization. Of course, there are many reasons why you might not work well with certain individuals, regardless of their gender. They may have 'shadows' – this means that they may remind you of people you have known in the past to whom you attribute negative or positive sexual or emotional feelings.

Curtail conflict Address issues of conflict with staff when sexual incidents have been reported to you.

Try using phrases like 'What I have observed. . . That makes me feel. . . What I need is. . .' This is mentioned in the section on how to deal with sexual liaisons between colleagues but it is also important to use this approach if you are dealing with the conflict of sexual incidents being reported to you. Get people to say exactly what they have *seen*, not what they have heard rumoured or reported. Ask them how they feel, not what they think, and do not accept 'I feel that you should do something about it' – that is not a feeling. That is a wish. 'I feel frustrated (unhappy, angry, anxious, frightened, hurt, scared, put down or embarrassed etc.) by their behaviour' would be a feeling. Then ask them what they need – 'I need them to be more professional.' This won't do. It is too woolly. Get them to be specific: 'I need them to work in different offices.' Then you have to have the skills to address the person who is creating the conflict because of a certain sexual incident. 'I have observed that you touch Susan's bottom when you are working at the desk. That makes me feel anxious. I need you to stop it.' You may want to talk about messages being misconstrued or suggest that Susan is consulted about the complaint, but it is important to be direct and precise as illustrated and not beat about the bush. Although the example is that of addressing a man, it could equally apply to a woman who you consider to be acting inappropriately.

Investigative interviews

In order to avoid unnecessary upsets amongst your staff which can demotivate and even end in industrial tribunals it is essential that your interviews are absolutely fair. If staff complain and consider that people have been appointed or promoted because of their sexual involvement with certain personnel then interviews will have to be investigated. So it is vital that proper procedures are followed not only because of sexual involvement or liaisons but in all cases. Baroness Blackstone, Education Minister, endorsed this view when interviewed in *Face the Facts* (September 1997). Complaints were received about a chief executive who appointed his mistress as his personal assistant. They later married and then she was promoted to head of personnel. According to the staff interviewed, this meant that any complaints or criticisms of him had to be channelled through his wife. The Baroness responded by saying that she was unfamiliar with the details of the case but in these situations the interviews would need to be investigated retrospectively. She commented that:

- the procedure had to comply with the law
- the job would have to be advertised
- the element of competition needed to be assessed
- a proper interview board had to be set up
- the partner should not take part in the interview

SO WHAT? HOW DOES THIS AFFECT ME AS A MANAGER?

So remember that when there are conflicts of interest and emotional associations then you have to be above reproach in any inquiry or investigation into the interview.

Summary

In terms of your organization, it is vital that you have guidelines of acceptable and non-acceptable behaviour. If you haven't got these then set up policies for 'sex' or 'love' at work. Establish an understanding and a formula with your staff about how they can complain if certain sexual relationships are affecting them or others at work.

Whilst in terms of managing your own sexuality:

- Remember that it is natural to have sexual feelings, but they may take up a lot of your psychic energy.
- Check out your feelings, if you feel uncomfortable in someone's presence it may be that they have a 'shadow' of someone you know or it may be because you are sexually attracted to them.
- Explore your attitudes towards sexuality and individuals. You may be attracted to someone but recognise the consequences of your becoming sexually involved with someone at work.
- Question your sexual feelings and the emotions that you may have towards other colleagues or customers and ask yourself if these feelings are affecting your decision making or working life.
- Treat yourself to further training on how to handle sexual issues at work.

SO WHAT? HOW DOES THIS AFFECT ME AS A MANAGER?

- Enjoy your sexuality. It is a vital element of your being.

FINAL CHECKLIST

S	Sexual feelings happen at work
E	Early sexual messages can affect people's sexual attitudes
X	Xplain that harassment will not be tolerated
U	Understand that staff have difficulties with sexuality between colleagues
A	Address complaints from staff about others' behaviour
L	Love is fine, lust is not
I	Implement a sexual harassment policy
T	Talk to staff when you believe their relationship is negatively affecting others
Y	You need to realise that some women staff may feel marginalised
A	Always be confidential about harassment disclosures
T	Try to relax when discussing items of a sexual nature. Listen with empathy to staff's concerns about sexual behaviour at work
W	Watch your language to prevent offence
O	Organise a policy that covers relationships at work
R	Remember that male and female chauvinism still exists
K	Keep a record of complaints about sexual issues.

FURTHER READING

1. Berne E (1974a) *Transactional analysis in psychotherapy*. Penguin
2. Berne E (1974b) *What do you say after you say Hello*. Penguin
3. Ellis A & Whiteley JM (1979) *Theoretical and empirical foundations of rational emotive therapy*. Brooks-Cole
4. Burrell G (1989) *The sexuality of organizations*. Sage
5. Boydell T & Hammond V (eds.) (1985) Men and Women in Organizations. *Management Education and Development 16* (2). Association of Teachers in Management
6. Hearn J et al. (1989) *The sexuality of organization*. Sage
7. Stone L (1977) *The family, sex and marriage in England 1500 – 1800*: Weidenfield & Nicolson
8. Rich A (1987) *Compulsory heterosexuality and lesbian existence*. Onlywomen Publishing
9. Friday N (1986) *Jealousy*. Collins
10. Dickson A (1985) *The mirror within: New Look at Sexuality*. Quartet
11. Zetterberg H (1966) *The Secret Ranking*. Journal of Marriage and the Family.
12. Harrison R & Lee R (1986) Love at Work. *Personnel Management* pp20-24
13. Burrell G (1984) *Sex and organizational analysis*. Organization Studies

14. Bradford DL et al. (1975) Executive man and woman: the issues of sexuality in bringing women into management. In *Bringing women into management* eds. FE Gordon & MH Strober. McGraw-Hill, N.Y
15. Kanter RM (1975) Women in organizations: sex roles, group dynamics and change strategies. In *Beyond sex roles* A. Sargent
16. Hochschild A (1983) *The managed heart: commercialisation or human feeling.* University of California
17. Rubin G (1984) Thinking Sex: notes for a radical; theory of the politics of sexuality. In *Pleasure and danger: exploring female sexuality.* CS Vance Routledge & Kegan Paul
18. Brake M (1982) Sexuality as Praxis – the consideration of the contribution of sexual theory to the process of sexual being. In *Human sexual relations* M Brake. Penguin
19. Gutek (1986) *Sex and the workplace, the impact of sexual behaviour and harassment on women, men and organizations.* Jossey-Bass
20. Quinn RE (1984) *Managing organization transition.* Homewood
21. Skynner R & Cleese J (1983) *Families and How to Survive Them.* Mandarin
21. ibid
22. Boydell T & M Pedler (1986) *Gender & work: guide materials for women and men in organizations.* Manpower Services Commission
23. Spender D (1980) *Man made language.* Routledge & Kegan Paul
24. Atkinson RL et al. (1990) *Introduction to psychology.* Tenth Ed. Harcourt Brace
25. Luria & Rubin (1982) The eye of the beholder: Parents view on sex of the newborns. *American Journal of Orthopsychiatry.*
26. Fineman S (1985) *Social work stress and intervention.* Gower Publishing

FURTHER READING

27. Pugh DS & Hickson DJ (1964) *Writers on Organizations.* Hutchinson
28. Perls F (1972) *In and out the garbage pail.* Bantam Books
29. Rogers C (1965) *Client centred therapy.* Constable, London
30. Torbett W (1992) *Managing the corporate dream: restructuring for long term success.* Homewood Dow-Jones/Irwin.
31. Quinn RE (1977) Coping with Cupid: the formation, impact and management of romantic relationships in organizations. *Administrative Science Quarterly* 22 pp 30-45
32. Collins EGC (1983) Managers and Lovers. *Havard Business Review* Vol 61 No. 5
33. Gray S (1984) Romance in the workplace: corporate rules for the game of love. *Business Week* 284-7, pp 70-1
34. Argyle M (1973) *Social interaction.* Tavistock publications
35. Jackall R (1988) *Moral mazes: The world of corporate managers.* Oxford Univ. Press
36. Cooper CH & Makin P (1983) *Psychology for managers at work.* Macmillan
37. Berne E (1968) *Games people play: the psychology of human relationships.* Penguin
38. Berne E (1973) *Sex in human loving.* Penguin
39. Hewson J & Turner CM (1992) *Transactional analysis in management.* The Staff College (now FEDA)
40 Turner CM (1992) Script analysis. The Staff College 1B paper.
41 Partington Geoffrey (1976) *Wommen Teachers in the Twentieth Century.* NFER
42. Rogers C (1970) *On becoming a person.* Constable
43. Rogers C (1978) *On personal power.* Constable
44 Hargreaves & Coley (1987) *The psychology of sex roles.* Harper & Row, London

45. Martin J et al. (1983) The uniqueness paradox in organizational stories. *Administrative Science quarterly*, Vol 28 No. 3 pp 438 – 453
46. van Maanen J (1988) *Tales of the field: on writing ethnography.* Univ of Chicago Press
47. Lyndon N (1992) *No more sex war.* Sinclair-Stevenson, London
48. Shakeshaft C (1990) Gender and Supervision. Conference Paper *Advances in Educational Management.* Vienna p. The Staff College.
49. Keller (1987) *The Gender/Science System or is Sex to Gender as Nature is to Science.*
50. Altman D et al. (1978) *Homosexuality – A study of diversity.* Allen Lane
51. Foucault M (1981) *The history of sexuality Vol 1 An introduction.* Penguin
52. Reason P & Rowan J (1988) *Human inquiry in action.* Sage
53. Steiner C M (1971) *Games alcoholics play.* Grave Press
54. Norwood R (1986) *Women who love too much.* Arrow Books
55. Steiner C (1975) *Scripts people live: Transactional analysis of life scripts.* Bantam
56. Glaser & Strauss (1979) *The discovery of grounded theory.* Aldine
57. Hite Shere (1976) Hite *Report on Female Sexuality*
58. Kaplan H (1975) *The new sex therapy.* Bailliere
59. Gillham (1991) *Child sexual abuse.* Cassell
60 Rollins J & White P N (1982) The relationship between mothers' and daughters' sex role attributes and self concepts in three types of family enviroment. *Sex Roles, 8, 1141-1155.*
61. O'Conner J & Seymour J (1990) *Introducing neurolinguistic programming: the new psychology of personal excellence.* Crucible.

INDEX

affairs, 25, 107-110, 112, 188, 194, 223
   case studies, 135-136, 137, 143-144,
      148-149, 154-156, 159, 162-163,
      175-176, 179
affection misconstrued, 113
ageism, 90, 226-227
aggressiveness, 23
AIDS see HIV
air hostesses, 36
applications, 26
appraisals, 207, *see also* interviews
assertiveness, 23
attitude changes
   analysis, 79-80, 128
   gender differences, 201
   male managers, 75-77
   men, 63, 181
   men not changing, 194
   women, 63
   women change more than men, 189
   women managers, 73-75
attractiveness, 95, 124, 141, 147, 177
author
   as counsellor, 21, 27-31, 197
   as management trainer, 21, 22-25
   as senior manager, 21, 25-27
   effect of research on, **195-202**

   surprised by some findings, 201
   work trivialised, 45
autosexual, 35, 174
battered babies, 28
bedroom promotion, 116
behaviour towards oppostie sex, 207
big boys don't cry, 63-64, 72, 79, 120,
      186, 190, 194
bisexual, 65, 174
blind eye syndrome, 110
boy wanted, girl arrived, 167, 171
bullying, sexual, 26

career vs children, 67-68, 156, 188
casting couch, 101, 104
Catholic Church, 69, 77-78, 126, 132,
      133, 139, 148, 162, 188
chauvinism
   female, 96, 104-105, 194
   male, 104, 194
childhood messages, 27, 54, 55, 90
children vs career, 67-68, 156, 188
chuff button, 186
civilisation concept, 45
cognitive dissonance, 139.
communication with opposite sex, 23
conclusions, **205-208**

INDEX

confesional tales, 107-110
conflict experienced, 77-79
counselling, 27-28, 224
courting conflict, 222
crumple button, 186
curtail conflict, 227-228
death and mourning, 186
depressives, 29
Dialectical research cycle, 198-199
Diana, Princess of Wales, 186
donít mix business with pleasure, 178
double standards, 45
downward power, 115-116
drugs dependency, 28-29, 30

early sexual messages, 28, 38, 53-56,
    59-60, 221
  analysis, 72, 128
  influence of, 30, 31
  male managers, 63-71
  women managers, 60-63
emotions of men, 43, 190, 194,
    see also big boys don't cry
equal opportunities, 23, 94, 96, 97-99,
    110-111, 176

false memory recall syndrome, 115
family impact, 54
feelings as facts, 0-192
female guile, 105, 194
feminism, 23, 105, 163
final checklist, 230
first sexual experiences
  abuse, 81, 82, 85-86
  ageism, 90
  analysis, 129

assault, 88-90
case studies, 133, 140,
    147-148, 153, 157-158, 161-162,
    165, 167-169, 172-174, 178
childhood messages, links with, 90
discovery, 87-88
full penetrative sex, 89-90
marriage, 83-84, 86-87, 193
masturbation, 83, 87
men, 86-90
orgasm, 82, 84-85
overview, 80-81
petting, 82-83
rape, 82, 85-86
summary, 91
women, 82-86, 88-90
flirting, 141
Further Education Development Agency,
    22

gay managers, 171
gender issues, 34, 55-56, 94-97
generation differences, 70-71, 105,
    226-227
guidelines essential, 229

high status person breaking rules, 147,
    152
Hite, Shere, 84-85
HIV, 62, 74, 76, 101-102, 176
homophobia, 63, 65
homosexuality, 22, 29-30, 65, 87,
    100-101, 111, 114, 125, 134,
    165-166, 226

INDEX

Id, 53, 54
inner conflict, 190-192
innuendos, sexual, 26, 97-98, 101
interviews, 17, 26, 103, 121-122, 124, 136, 142-143, 148-149 170, 176, 187-188, 192-193, 207, 228-229
Islam, 45, 51

Johari window theory, 142
Joyless messages, 29

legal aspects of management, 191
lesbianism, 29-30, 100, 114, 226
liaisons strain loyalty, 223
lingerie embarrassment, 75
love, need for, 24
loyalty strained by liaisons, 223
Lucretia Borgia types, 144-145
macho image, 59, 63, 64, 76, 79, 95, 105, 124, 152, 194
male managers
　attitude changes, 75-77
　early sexual messages, 63-71
　liaisons at work, 27
　sexual messages at work, 94-102, 104-106
　values and belief systems, 26
managerial fairness, 171
　influence of sexuality, 53-56
　early sexual messages, 30
managing your own sexuality, **221-230**
marriage memories, 60-61
masturbation, 68
maternity leave, 68
meetings, 119-120, 188, 222-223

men
　fear of showing feelings, 23
　multiple roles, 24
　mixing business with pleasure, 99
Ms factor, 26

nominal men, 98
nominal women, 98

organization messages and stories, conclusions, 207-208
O.R.G.A.S.M., 132

paedophiles, 168-169
patriarchal ethos, 25
permanent prejudices, 222
positive discrimination, 97-98
potent power, 225
power and equality, 76
pregnancy, 67-68, 134-135, 188, 189
preventive policies, 224
Prima Gravida organization, 96
prisons and prisoners, 29-30, 52-53, 102, 160
promotions, 112, 115-116, 118-119, 124, 176-177
psychic energy, 27, 46
punishments, 51

questionnaires
　mailing address, 215
　manager as role model, 210-212
　personal, 57-59
　preliminary, 19-20
　sexuality of others, 214-215
　sexuality of the manager, 212-213

INDEX

racist discrimination, 180
realistic tales, 110-114
recalled sexual messages, 18-19
red lampshade, 83
religious morality, 45
religious teaching, 188,
    see also Catholic Church research
research
    academic relevance, 46, 203, 205
    affect on author, **195-202**
    affect on researcher, 47
    background, 15-16
    case studies - later developments, 183-185
    case studies - reasons, 181-183
    case studies - summary, 185-186
    closed organizations, 52-53
    competence steps, 200
    confidentiality, 200-201
    counselling aspect, 20
    Dailectical research cycle, 198-199
    difficulties, 30
    educational relevance, 205
    framework, 196-197
    funding, 46-47
    introduction, 31-32
    limited previous work, 205
    management relevance, 203-204, 205
    motives, **21-32**
    open organizations, 52-53
    practical significance, 202
    previous, **41-56**
    Rowan's Research cycle, 197-199
    therapeutic community relevance, 204
Rowan's Research cycle, 197-199
rule breaking by high status people, 115-116

script analysis, 54-55
scripting, 29
scripts, 54, 55
Second World War, 50
sex
    conflicting messages, 61
    discussion avoided, 66, 70-71, 78, 190
    embarrassing, 62-63
    enjoyable, 61
    enjoyable - but, 66
    love, 66-67, 135
    marriage, 188, 193
    men as docile partners, 108
    modesty, 62-63
    naughty but nice, 133
    negative messages, 68
    nice after all, 74
    nice girls don't, 60, 188
    not nice, 60-61
    power, 78
    powerful, 123
    sin, 69
    to be endured, 61
    women's use to gain power, 111
sex role, 55-56
sex stereotyping, 69-70, 94-97, 157
sex typing, 55-56, 69-70, 76, 122-123, 194
sexist remarks, 114
sexual attitudes, 55, 206
sexual essentialism, 36
sexual harassment, 111, 113, 175, 225
    10 managers' rules, 218-219
    EC code, 216-217
    guidelines for managers, 216-219
    manager's role, 215-216, 219-221
    Siller's Gentlemen's Rules, 217-218

INDEX

sexual liaisons, 51-52
sexual messages at work
  analysis, 106, 129
  male managers, 94-102, 104-106
  patterns, 93-94
  stories, 106-107
  women managers, 94-104
sexual passion18
sexual projection, 122-123
sexual stereotyping, 100, 121, 125, 188, 206-207
sexual stories at work, 117, 130, 223-224
sexual underlife of organizations, 44, 45
sexuality
  academic attitude, 46
  affect on male managers, 118-121, 122-123, 123-126
  affect on women managers, 118-122, 123-126
  analysis of affect, 127, 130
  definitions, **33-40**
  definitions broadened, 37-38
  definitions neither right nor wrong, 38
  denial of, 17
  emotions of, 21
  historic problems, 51
  historical view, 34
  impact on work, **117-130**
  influence on managers, 53-56
  male power base, 61
  masculine interpretations, 37
  not left at home, 43
  partnership basis, 38
  perceptions, 36
  political, 35
  power of, 35, 46

privacy of, 35, 36, 43
public process, 34-35
punishments, 51
repressed, 51
states [list], 39
taboo subject, 44-45
sexuality at work
  control required, 50-53
  inner conflict, 190-192
  manager's perceptions, **93-130**
  past research, **41-56**
  psychodynamics, 50-53
  quantitative studies, 42-43
  used by women, 109-110
space protected, 113
Staff College, 22
stoning to death, 45, 51

taboo subject, 44-45
teaching profession, 67-68
temptresses, 70
Thatcher, Lady, 105
touching people, 97-98, 136, 137
transactional analysis, 28, 54
turn a blind eye syndrome, 52

uniqueness paradox, 107
upward power, 115-116

value for money, 46
Victorian beliefs, 45
women
  clever, 154
  marginalised by men, 94, 103-104
  multiple roles, 24
  patronized, 95
  senior management, 24

INDEX

Women into Management conferences, 24
women managers
  attitude changes, 73-75
  early sexual messages, 60-63
  sexual messages at work, 94-104